4·17·79

THE
SEPARATE
PROBLEM

THE
SEPARATE
PROBLEM

Case Studies
of Black Education
in the North,
1900-1930

Judy Jolley Mohraz

CONTRIBUTIONS IN AFRO-AMERICAN
AND AFRICAN STUDIES, NUMBER 42

Greenwood Press
Westport, Connecticut • London, England

Library of Congress Cataloging in Publication Data

Mohraz, Judy Jolley.
    The separate problem.

    (Contributions in Afro-American and African
studies ; no. 42 ISSN 0069-9624)
    Bibliography: p.
    Includes index.
    1. Afro-Americans—Education—History.
2. Segregation in education—United States—
History. I. Title. II. Series.
LC 2801.M6   270'.973   78-4026
ISBN 0-313-20411-X

Library of Congress Catalog Card Number: 78-4026
ISBN: 0-313-20411-X
ISSN: 0069-9624

First published in 1979

Greenwood Press, Inc.
51 Riverside Avenue, Westport, Connecticut 06880

Printed in the United States of America

10 9 8 7 6 5 4 3 2 1

2045464

To
Claire and Jim

CONTENTS

ACKNOWLEDGMENTS

In the course of the research and writing of this study, I have had the privilege of guidance and advice from some remarkably supportive as well as able scholars. To David B. Tyack of Stanford University who introduced me to this area of challenging research and whose encouragement and help enabled me to pursue this study, I am especially indebted. Winton U. Solberg of the University of Illinois offered me invaluable assistance through his attention to problems of organization and clarity as well as content, and I gratefully acknowledge his help. Special thanks are also extended to R. Hal Williams of Southern Methodist University who provided vital aid in the final stages of preparation of the manuscript.

I am also grateful to August Meier for his excellent suggestions as well as to Paul Violas, Robert Harris, Robert McColley, and J. Leonard Bates for their constructive comments on an earlier draft. While any strengths of this book are in large part the result of their incisive criticism, all defects and shortcomings are mine alone.

Two typists, Katherine Patton and Vickie Dunnam, typed the manuscript with good humor as well as skill.

Finally, several generations of my family—my parents, my husband Bijan, and our son Andrew—are deeply appreciated for their sustained support, assistance, and, in the case of Andrew, abstinence from rearranging my desk. I trust that the dedication of this book to Claire and Jim Quicksall suggests some degree of the depth of my gratitude to them.

Judy Jolley Mohraz

INTRODUCTION

The problems and needs in Negro education were the topics of numerous articles and studies in magazines and educational journals at the turn of the century. In almost all cases, however, the northern philanthropists and educators who discussed the issues considered Negro education to be a southern problem, and they paid little attention to the schooling of black children in burgeoning urban areas in the North. During the same period, progressive schoolmen, administrators, and civic groups, led by the urban gentry, redefined the role of the school and transformed it into a prime agent in the socialization of immigrants. Yet, they, too, were curiously silent about the function of the educational system in incorporating Afro-American children into twentieth-century America. While the Negro students in the North remained "the invisible ones," their numbers were increasing, even before the influx of southern blacks during World War I, and their experiences and difficulties would have justified studies and policies related to their needs.

Only after the Negroes inundated northern industrial centers during the second decade of the century did these black students become visible to many schoolmen. The educators' response frequently was to approach the issue of Negroes in the schools with the question "What is the Negro's problem in the schools?" One can observe this attitude in an early study of black students in Philadelphia which Howard Odum made for the Philadelphia Bureau of Municipal Research. "Negro pupils," Odum contended in the 1913 report, "constitute a separate problem of education in the schools."[1] Despite the educators' perception of Negro education as a separate problem, many of the conditions which hindered the scholastic progress of black children, such as detrimental neighborhood conditions, poor health, and few economic advantages (discussed in Chapter 2), were problems confronting white lower-class children as well. Moreover, to pose the question in terms of the Negro's problem was, as William Ryan said, "to blame the victim."[2]

In fact, black education only became "a separate problem" because many educators believed the Negro student needed a special type of education and separate schools. Thus, an important question historians must consider is "Why did early twentieth-century schoolmen perceive Negro education as demanding separate policies?" Another vital question which educators refused to address is "What was the school's problem?" Why did the school so often fail to serve these clients adequately?

When studies critical of the schools' policies toward the Negro did appear, they frequently dealt with rather narrow questions such as to what extent segregation existed in the North or what kind of discrimination black children encountered. These questions are important, and Chapters 5 and 6 attempt to describe the extent and type of segregation and discrimination confronting the black student. They show the way discriminatory policies developed and matured, establishing by 1930 the means educators would use for many years to maintain racial separation and inequality in the schools. However, one may gain more perspective on the educational experiences of the Negro by considering these issues within a broader framework. One needs to ask such questions as what kind of institution was the new twentieth-century urban school? Who designed it to serve what purposes? What practices did schoolmen introduce to realize these goals? And, finally, how did schoolmen view their largest group of clients, lower class children?

Chapters 3 and 4 present evidence that certain educational policies and goals introduced in progressive urban school systems before 1930 were inherently discriminatory against blacks and other low socioeconomic groups. These programs which educators proclaimed as reforms, such as intelligence testing, ability grouping, and differentiated curricula, produced a type of class education which directly affected Negro students. Thus, in part, one needs to consider the consequences of educational reform in the early twentieth century rather than to limit the analysis to black educational practices alone.

The policies of three cities, Philadelphia, Indianapolis, and Chicago, are analyzed in an attempt to delineate the contours of black education in northern public schools from the end of the nineteenth century to

1930. The dilemmas and problems of black communities, as well as
administrators' attitudes and white citizens' prejudices, are considered.
These cities were selected because they provide important contrasts as
well as similarities in the forces which molded the position of the schools
toward black students. The similarities include the existence in all three
cities of discrimination by the educational system against Negroes. However, each city used different devices to implement varying degrees of
segregation and unequal treatment of these children. Another common
factor among the cities was the development of intensified discrimination
after World War I which was triggered by the massive migration of southern
blacks into these urban areas.

   The Negro communities' lack of power, both politically and economically,
was an obvious condition which allowed discriminatory policies to exist.
In no city did blacks possess the economic power to combat racism; however, in Chicago, Negroes did attain a significant degree of political power.
Thus, a study of this city provides an opportunity to determine to what
extent political power could deter unequal treatment in a politically controlled school system. Linked with this political power was a common commitment by the city's blacks to the maintenance of integrated schools.
This consensus was in marked contrast to some other northern black communities torn between segregated schools which provided employment for
Negroes and mixed schools which barred black teachers. Nevertheless,
Chicago's education history during these years demonstrates the inability
of black political power alone to produce equal education. It also points
up the difficulty of blocking subtle de facto segregation in a city waging
battle to restrict Negroes to a congested Black Belt.

   In all of these cities white prejudice influenced school policy, but
Indianapolis provides the best example of the existence of the militant
racism generally associated with the South. The concept of a rigid dual
system sanctioned by law evokes images of southern educational practices,
but a study of Indianapolis indicates that de jure segregation has had national rather than regional dimensions. Indianapolis provides another
important insight: an accommodationist stance by a black community
could not blunt white reaction and racism. Repression occurred whether
a black community eschewed militance, as in Indianapolis, or endorsed
activism, as in Chicago. An analysis of Indianapolis schools is also valuable
because its educational system was hailed shortly before 1900 as one of
the finest in the nation.[3] Yet, this was the system which sanctioned greater
dilution of the academic curriculum for Negroes than either of the other

two cities. No educational leader assailed Indianapolis's curriculum policies or dealt with the inequality of the black students' education.

Philadelphia was selected because here, unlike Indianapolis, Chicago, and other northern cities which Negroes inundated in the war years, blacks had been an integral and visible part of the community for over two hundred years. This study suggests that the sudden appearance of significant numbers of blacks precipitated substantial white reaction and increased discrimination in a northern city. Despite the Negro's deep roots in Philadelphia, however, he was the victim of the same type of heightened discrimination that his brothers in other cities endured. Philadelphia also illustrates the painful dilemma black citizens faced when their race was barred from teaching in mixed schools. The division of the city's black leadership over the issue of mixed versus separate schools illuminates the reasons Negroes often disagreed about the issue.

In considering the question of segregation, one assumption in this study should be noted: segregation produced inferior education for black children because of inadequate facilities and frequently diluted academic programs. Mixed classes, on the other hand, generally offered better facilities and a stronger academic curriculum. Most Negroes working for integration during the period included in this study were motivated by this reason rather than the contention that white and black interaction in the schools would produce more racial understanding and tolerance. But one should observe that some black educators and leaders, including W.E.B. DuBois, began to question the desirability of integrated schools by the 1930s. They saw their children fail and drop out in larger numbers in mixed schools than in separate ones staffed by sympathetic black teachers. Thus, by 1935, DuBois proclaimed that the psychological damage inflicted on black children through discrimination in integrated schools outweighed the advantages of integration.[4] DuBois' position brought an end to his association with the NAACP, an organization committed to the philosophy finally accepted by the federal government in the 1954 *Brown* v. *Board of Education* decision.

This study also embodies another assumption: the schools had a responsibility to attempt to alter the status quo in a prejudiced society. While American education could not purge the nation of three hundred years of racism, it could have tried to effect more change in the Negro's position in American society than it did. Instead, as this study shows, the schools reinforced the status quo and failed to be instruments of reform. This fact becomes even more significant when it is compared to the myth that

schoolmen, earlier historians, and the public have embraced—that the
public schools have been the chief vehicle of democracy. Colin Greer de-
scribes what he calls "the great school legend" as the contention that the
schools "took the backward poor, the ragged, ill-prepared ethnic minorities
who crowded into the cities, educated and Americanized them into the
homogeneous middle class that is America's strength and pride."[5] A new
body of educational history presents evidence of the fallacy of this characterization of American education in the late nineteenth and early twentieth centuries.[6]

As historians have begun to trace the experience of lower class children
in the schools, manifold problems have hampered the research. The difficulty becomes even greater in approaching one facet of lower class education—that of the schooling of black children—because the material is frequently scant or nonexistent.[7] Black schoolchildren left few records of
their experience in the classroom. Administrators and school boards were
careful in cities such as Philadelphia and Chicago to veil discriminatory
policies and to avoid acknowledging them in official records. Vital records
of the early twentieth-century school systems have frequently been destroyed—either intentionally or inadvertently as superintendents changed,
as boards of education moved from one building to another, and as storage
space was exhausted. White newspapers throughout the period neglected
coverage of the black community or concentrated on stories related to
black crime or sensational scandals, not on educational issues.[8] Therefore,
this study has had to rely heavily on black newspaper accounts of school
policies since no other sources are extant. However, when one reads the
Chicago Commission on Race Relations' study of educational policies in
that city preceding the 1919 riot or other official reports on education
in the various cities, one concludes that the accounts of educational discrimination which the *Philadelphia Tribune* or the *Chicago Defender*
printed were not atypical.

Nevertheless, many important questions go unanswered or only partially
answered. Some important issues yet to be explored include the way educational theory affected the individual classroom; the reasons progressive
educators did not deal with black needs to any significant extent; and
whether decentralized systems administered by ward boards in the nineteenth century provided Negroes with any more influence than they had
when dealing with twentieth-century centralized systems.

The provocative new research in educational history in the past few
years has begun to provide insights into related issues such as the impact

of bureaucratization, elite control, and class education, which have important implications for understanding not only urban educational history but also black education. The scholarship has also, in Michael Katz's words, given contemporary Americans "a realistic and usable educational past—one that shows how the current situation, with all its faults, came to be."[9] It is hoped that this study of the problems, dilemmas, and experiences of northern blacks and the urban school systems in three cities during a transition period will give further historical perspective to the background of the contemporary crisis in urban education.

NOTES

1. Howard W. Odum, "Negro Children in the Public Schools of Philadelphia," *Annals of the American Academy of Political and Social Science* 49 (September 1913): 197.

2. William Ryan, *Blaming the Victim* (New York: Vintage Books, 1971), Ch. 2.

3. J. M. Rice, "The Public Schools of St. Louis and Indianapolis," *Forum* 14 (December 1892): 429-444.

4. W.E.B. DuBois, "Does the Negro Need Separate Schools," *Journal of Negro Education* 4 (July 1935): 328-335.

5. Colin Greer, *The Great School Legend* (New York: Basic Books, 1972), pp. 3-4.

6. For example, see David B. Tyack, *The One Best System: A History of American Urban Education* (Cambridge, Mass.: Harvard University Press, 1974); Michael B. Katz, *Class, Bureaucracy and Schools* (New York: Praeger Publishers, 1971); Clarence J. Karier, ed., *Shaping the American Educational State: 1900 to the Present* (New York: Free Press, 1975); Clarence J. Karier, Paul C. Violas, and Joel Spring, eds., *Roots of Crisis: American Education in the Twentieth Century* (Chicago: Rand McNally and Co., 1973); and Robert Wiebe, "The Social Function of Public Education," *American Quarterly* 21 (Summer 1969): 147-164.

7. While a small percentage of black children in the North were from middle-class families, the number was too small, and the proportion of black students from lower class backgrounds so great, that this study generally considers black education as one aspect of lower class education.

8. See Frederick G. Detweiler, *The Negro Press in the United States* (Chicago: University of Chicago Press, 1922), and George Eaton Simpson, *The Negro in the Philadelphia Press* (Philadelphia: University of Pennsylvania Press, 1936) for analysis of newspaper coverage of black issues.

9. Michael B. Katz, ed., *Education in American History* (New York: Praeger Publishers, 1973), p. viii.

THE
SEPARATE
PROBLEM

1 THE BLACK EXPERIENCE IN THREE CITIES

By 1900, race relations in every northern metropolitan center were deteriorating. The attention directed to the black American's condition during Reconstruction had softened some of the oppression and discrimination Negroes had endured, but northern white support for black political rights was not coupled with commitment to social equality and fraternity.[1] Nothing in the history of the Northerners' treatment of Negroes in their own region had laid the foundation for the sanction of equality. The Negro living in the antebellum North was generally disfranchised, segregated, and economically subjugated,[2] and nineteenth-century racial prejudices continued to restrict the northern black after the war.[3] Humanitarian concern for the Negro by the Republican party in the Reconstruction era was interlaced with political motivation, and in the decades following Reconstruction, selfish political considerations dominated party policy on the Negro question. By 1893, the issue of Negro rights was no longer politically expedient to the Republicans. Therefore, the party abandoned the Negro and left him to make his way alone in a nation marked by racial apathy or hostility.[4]

White indifference or muted resentment to the Negro placed the northern black in a precarious position. An uncertain peace between the races was maintained as long as the Negro's numbers were few and interracial contact minimal. However, the rising percentage of Negroes in northern cities in the last decades of the nineteenth century altered the previous obscurity of the black residents and triggered varying degrees of racial hostility and tension. Heightened friction followed the greater visibility of Negroes in the early twentieth-century city—on the streets, in residential areas, on the job, and in the schools.

Discrimination accompanied the hostility and confronted the Negro in all aspects of his life, forcing him into the bottom layer of urban society. His inferior position in the social, economic, and political sectors was also reflected in the educational sphere. Therefore, in order to understand the Negro experience in the northern school, one must make at least a cursory delineation of the broader urban scene in the three cities included in this study.

Certain common characteristics existed in Indianapolis, Philadelphia, and Chicago at the turn of the century. Each was an industrial and cultural center of its state. All of them were pressing their boundaries far beyond nineteenth-century city limits as they swelled with new industries, increased commerce, and exploding populations. Each struggled to provide additional municipal services for their growing numbers. And each grappled to adjust to the heterogeneity of their new residents—a significant number of whom were black.

PHILADELPHIA

Philadelphia, the historic City of Brotherly Love, had a long and disparate history related to its black residents. One strand of the black Philadelphians' experience suggested a notable degree of concern and awareness of the Negro among whites. Blacks had been a visible group in the community from the colonial period onward. They possessed a certain degree of financial security according to W.E.B. DuBois, who estimated that until about 1820 a majority of Philadelphia's artisans were black.[5] The Quakers had sympathized with the plight of the Negro, and by 1780 the Act for the Gradual Abolition of Slavery was law. Concerned with education for black residents, the Quakers began an integrated school in the eighteenth century.

Philadelphia was a center for both white and black abolition efforts. It witnessed the first Negro convention in 1830 at the Bethel Church and the founding of the American Anti-Slavery Society in 1833. Following the Civil War, some prominent Philadelphians remained concerned with the conditions of Negro citizens, and one of these civic leaders encouraged the University of Pennsylvania in the 1890s to initiate the first extensive study of Negroes in a northern city. The university selected the young

black scholar W.E.B. DuBois to make the survey, and the classic study
The Philadelphia Negro resulted.

While black Philadelphians suffered from housing restrictions in the
pre-World War I city, a study of ten northern cities has revealed that
this Pennsylvania city had a smaller degree of residential segregation in
1910 than seven other urban areas, including Chicago, Boston, and Cincinnati.[6] Blacks gained admittance to most public facilities before the
Great Migration, and some residents described the pre-World War I racial
situation favorably.[7]

Yet, there was another darker strand of Negro experience in Philadelphia. From the early nineteenth century, Negroes had experienced
sporadic harassment, but in 1834 anti-Negro sentiment and resentment
of abolitionists' efforts exploded in a race riot which left Negro areas
pitted by white vandalism. In 1838 and 1842, further riots directed against
the Negroes and the abolitionists swept the city. As a consequence, Negroes
lost economic power and many moved from Philadelphia. By 1850, the
city's black population had decreased for the first time in census history.[8]
Sam Bass Warner, Jr., noting this white hostility to Negroes, suggests that
"in respect to Negro caste practices, Philadelphia was a southern city,
and Philadelphia Negroes 'knew their place.' "[9] After the war, resentment
of Negro voting power, particularly by the Irish community, precipitated
the murder in 1871 of a black teacher in a street fight on election day.
This incident shocked the city to such an extent that leading citizens began
to make special efforts to alleviate tension and remove barriers to Negroes
in places of public accommodation.[10]

By 1890, the Negro population had increased to 39,371 of the total
population of 1,046,964, making Philadelphia the northern city with the
largest black community. This figure represented 3.76 percent of the total
city population.[11] Within this community, some Negroes had established
economic and social security, and a small but influential number of upper
class Negroes constituted perhaps the largest group of successful blacks in
the nation.[12] But the number of successful Negroes did not mean that
the Negro community would have the necessary leadership in order to
combat racial prejudice, which became more prevalent in the early twentieth century. For if Philadelphia whites had a strong sense of caste, the
same social stratification operated in black Philadelphia as well. In 1896,
DuBois wrote about the possible three thousand Negroes who formed the
upper class of the Negro population: "They are not the leaders or the

ideal makers of their own group. . . . They teach the masses to a very small extent, mingle with them but little, do not hire their labor."[13] These "Old Philadelphians," those who were natives of the city or had lived there for a long time and had attained social and economic prestige, were divided among themselves as to how they should promote racial justice and often exhibited only negligible race consciousness.

In 1927, the Negro newspaper the *Philadelphia Tribune* contrasted Chicago's civil rights and racial gains with the less impressive progress Philadelphia had realized. The *Tribune* complained that "there is as much intelligence among Negroes in Philadelphia as there are [sic] in Chicago. There are perhaps more wealthy colored citizens in Philadelphia than in the middle-western city." The editorial attributed the difference to the sense of racial unity and cooperation in Chicago as contrasted to the individuality and division of Philadelphia Negroes.[14] Black cohesion in Philadelphia was also deterred by the existence of three major black areas in the city, and Negroes were unable to promote separate black businesses and services to the degree Afro-Americans had in cities with monolithic black enclaves.[15] In fact, by 1930, the Philadelphia Negro community had a smaller percentage of black retail dealers among its population than Chicago and a smaller proportion of its residents in professional fields such as law and medicine than either Chicago or Indianapolis.[16]

An even greater sense of division within the Negro community occurred as migration increased. The black population rose over 63 percent from 1890 to 1900. It surged from 62,613, or 4.84 percent, of the city population in 1900 to 84,469, or 5.45 percent, in 1910 (see Table 1). By 1920, it had skyrocketed to 134,229, which constituted 7.37 percent of all Philadelphia residents. Further increases followed in the 1920s, and by 1930, 219,599 Philadelphians were black, or over eleven out of every one hundred residents.[17] Many of the migrants arriving during and after World War I came not from the upper South, a frequent place of origin of many earlier newcomers, but from the Carolinas and Georgia, states whose poverty and illiteracy levels were higher than those in the upper South. For example, in 1910 the illiteracy rate among Negroes in Georgia and South Carolina was 36.5 and 38.7 percent, respectively. This level of illiteracy was in contrast to Maryland, where only 23.4 percent of the Negro residents were in this category, or to Pennsylvania, which had only 9.1 percent illiteracy among its black citizens.[18]

Table 1

Negro Population of Philadelphia 1890-1930

Date	Total Population	Negro Population	Percent Negro
1890	1,046,964	39,371	3.76
1900	1,293,697	62,613	4.84
1910	1,549,008	84,469	5.45
1920	1,823,779	134,229	7.37
1930	1,950,961	219,599	11.22

SOURCE: *U.S. Census Reports,* 1890-1930.

Each increase in black numbers in the city caused more white reaction and curtailment of Negro rights.[19] Consequently, upper class Negroes viewed the influx of illiterate southern Negroes as undermining all the advancements the race had made in the past.[20]

Yet, the existence of this established community of relatively educated and settled Negroes made some observers theorize that the migrants' adjustment in Philadelphia would be easier than in other cities.[21] To some degree, this may have occurred—no major race riots scarred the city in the tumultuous summer of 1919—but for the average migrant, the resentment of established blacks as well as the hostility of white Philadelphians made adjustment difficult. Furthermore, divisions among the elite concerning strategy for racial advancement, particularly in the area of segregated versus desegregated schools, undermined community cohesion.

All parts of the black community, however, were united on one issue— that of political allegiance to the Republican party. The Republican machine predominated, despite occasional onslaughts from elite reform groups which charged that Republican control had produced corruption as well as inefficiency in city politics. Philadelphia Negroes were unswerving supporters of the party of Lincoln and therefore did not have to be courted to any significant extent by the politicians. Political apathy and lack of organization prevailed in the black community, and Philadelphia Negroes never developed the power in the political arena which Chicago

Negroes attained. In 1927, the *Tribune* assailed its brothers' political apathy by noting that "we have the vast majority of the votes in the Thirtieth Ward, but we permit an illiterate and hostile white man to boss it and a few of his hirelings to run it."[22] A later study of Philadelphia black politicians made a similar assessment of black acquiescence in politics during this period, when it termed the Negro's role in the city's politics as "passive . . . not because it had to be, but rather because he allowed it to be."[23]

Philadelphia Negroes—and blacks and urban lower classes in general—remained committed to the political machine system, despite the few rewards it provided to the black community. They refused to support reform movements spearheaded by upper class groups attempting to seize power from ward bosses and machine politicians. Reformers could not promise Negroes jobs—blacks believed ward heelers could. And it was these coveted jobs as policemen and city workers that the black community needed. DuBois explained that "Negroes had always been suspicious that the reform movement tended not to their betterment but to their elimination from political life and consequently from the best chance of earning a living."[24] Furthermore, Negroes felt little affinity with reformers who swarmed into black neighborhoods only before elections. "When the apostles of civil reform compete with [*sic*] the ward Boss in friendliness and kind consideration for the unfortunate," DuBois asserted, ". . . then we can expect the more rapid development of civic virtue in the Negro and indeed in the whole city."[25]

Negroes frequently complained that "reform governments" discriminated against the black race, even when the appointments were made on the basis of merit. In 1914, the *Tribune* criticized the reform administration which had overturned Republican machine control for discriminating against Negro office seekers. It charged that "civil service rules are discarded" because when Negroes received notification to fill a certain job and city officials discovered they were black, excuses were made for not hiring them.[26]

Municipal political reform was not the only focus of the elite. Educational reform also came from the top and bypassed the Negro.[27] DuBois suggested that in this area as in municipal politics, blacks, even upper class blacks, could not support a movement which would remove whatever minor influence they might have through political channels.[28] As in municipal politics, reformers were not attuned to black needs. For example, the Public Education Association, an elite reform organization dedicated to improving Philadelphia schools, appeared unaware of the needs of the substantial number of Negroes in the schools or of the issues of discrimination and segregation. In 1914, the association published a report entitled *A Generation of Progress in Our Public Schools, 1881-1912*. In listing the main interests and efforts of the organization during the thirty-year period, nothing related to Negroes was included.[29]

The school board was even more disinclined to attack problems related to Negro students than the Public Education Association. In 1911, the school board was decreased in size and removed from political influence. The judges of the courts of common pleas of Philadelphia, themselves chosen by the governor, were assigned the duty of appointing the fifteen members of the board for six-year terms, which were generally automatically renewed. In contrast to the nineteenth-century ward school boards which had included laborers, janitors, trolley car motormen, and watchmen on the governing bodies, the single, citywide school board consisted of upper and upper middle-class businessmen and professionals.[30] Educational reformers hailed this reorganization and the resulting change in leadership as providing more efficient and professional school administration. One educator approved of the elite composition of the board because "the nature of the occupation may determine the ordinary morality of the individual."[31] The consequences of the reorganization, however, did not benefit the black community. Negroes found the new educational policy-makers unresponsive to black protests against discrimination and supportive of further segregation.

The board of education's discriminatory position toward Negro students and teachers reflected a common attitude of the majority of white Philadelphians. Negroes faced employment barriers in the city similar to those existing for all black Americans. Just before the turn of the century, 90 percent of blacks living in the seventh ward in Philadelphia were servants and laborers, compared with a city average in these occupations of 46.8 percent.[32] In some fields of employment such as machine shops, textile industries, and the new electrical supply manufactures, the Negro was completely excluded even in the 1920s.[33] Nor would labor unions welcome black membership. DuBois reported on the subtle but effective means by which Philadelphia unions disbarred Negroes. In an interview with the vice-president of the Philadelphia Federation of Labor in the late 1890s, the labor leader explained to DuBois that the federation allowed Negroes in any of its trade unions. He also stated, however, that while a majority of union members were willing to admit blacks, a powerful minority opposed admission. Therefore, though no formal opposition would occur during discussion, members would quietly veto admission in voting.[34] Unions were also able to exclude blacks from certain industries. In 1931, Sterling Spero and Abram Harris reported that it was almost impossible for black plumbers to work in Philadelphia. The licensing board in the city, which had union representatives on it, refused to license Negro plumbers.[35] Despite the inroads in industry which Philadelphia Negroes made during the war years, a 1927 survey reported that the city's Negroes were still employed primarily in domestic and personal service.[36] Furthermore, during the first three decades of the century, blacks lost ground in commercial fields such as catering and barbering, which they had previously dominated.[37]

The relatively small outlet for middle-class Negroes in political jobs and black businesses may explain why many Philadelphia blacks were willing to accept separate black schools. These schools offered professional status and jobs for black teachers who were barred from teaching in the mixed or white schools of the city.

Negroes also faced restrictions when they attempted to use public facilities. In the older areas of Philadelphia, public playgrounds were open to Negroes. In other areas where blacks lived in large numbers, public recreational centers and swimming pools refused to admit Negroes.[38] Semipublic facilities also frequently refused to open their doors to blacks. Thus, social settlements, community centers, and YMCA and YWCA branches either segregated Negroes or did not offer them their services.[39]

Housing restrictions were even more rigid. In 1921, one Philadelphia study charged that "the newly built modern house was not for rent or for sale to Negroes."[40] The confrontation which came closest to being a race riot in the city developed because a black municipal court officer moved into a white neighborhood in 1918. White neighbors besieged the house, and an imbroglio ensued which left two dead and sixty injured.[41] One of the most important consequences of the great influx of blacks into the city was the spiralling residential segregation. White opposition to integrated neighborhoods became so effective that between 1920 and 1930 racial separation in housing increased by more than 32 percent.[42]

Promotion of racial understanding received little attention from important groups in the white community. Civic leaders seldom spoke out on
the issue, and religious leaders were not active in attempts to curtail discrimination. The Catholic church, for example, channeled its efforts into
separate black parishes and grade schools for the two thousand Negro
Catholics in Philadelphia. Rather than open white parochial schools to
more than a few black children, four separate black parochial schools
educated six hundred Negro elementary pupils.[43] White churches provided
little aid for needy migrants during World War I, and almost all help from
religious sources came from black churches. Yet, the newcomer was often
not welcome in established Negro churches, and several churches split
over the admission of illiterate southern migrants.[44]

White newspapers not only refused to attack racial prejudice in the
city but also reinforced white hostility toward the Negro. George E.
Simpson surveyed the way four leading newspapers dealt with Negro
news items and concluded that the articles were often prejudiced and
detrimental to racial harmony.[45] Furthermore, the news about Negroes
carried in the papers decreased in the period 1908 to 1932, despite the
186 percent increase in the black population during this time.[46] When
whites did read about black activity, the news items were generally related to Negro crime. Only one-fourth of all published material about
blacks concerned such issues as education, religion, health, science,
and economic activities.[47]

Several black newspapers in the city, including the nationally circulated *Tribune*, worked for racial justice; however, readership of Negro
periodicals and weekly newspapers was limited to members of the black
community. Chris J. Perry, who founded the *Tribune* in 1884 and edited
it until his death in 1921, attempted to foster racial pride and publicize
cases of racial discrimination.[48] But the *Tribune* frequently failed to
mobilize the fragmented black community to attack injustices and did
not have the impact on the Philadelphia Negro community which the
Defender achieved among Chicago blacks.

Thus, Philadelphia, despite its significant percentage of black residents,
regardless of the Negro's long tradition in the city, and in defiance of
civil rights laws in the state, was not prepared to deal equitably with
Negro citizens. And the lack of cohesion among Negroes made them highly
vulnerable to the prejudices embedded in economic, political, and social
institutions.

INDIANAPOLIS

The historic Mason-Dixon line along Indiana's southern border marked it as a northern state. Yet, southern racial values cast a heavy shadow over the Hoosier state. Exclusion of Negroes from Indiana was a popular sentiment in the antebellum period, and legislation deterring Negroes from settling there passed the legislature and was upheld by the state supreme court in 1862.[49] In the years following the Civil War, attempts to exclude the freedman continued, but some Negroes were undaunted: between 1860 and 1890, the state's black population rose from 11,428 to 45,215.[50] By 1890, 9,154 Negroes had settled in Indianapolis, the state capital, and the number grew to 15,963 by the beginning of the century, an increase of over 15,500 in the forty-year period[51] (see Table 2). Only Philadelphia, New York, St. Louis, Chicago, Kansas City, and Pittsburgh had larger black populations among northern cities. More important, in 1900, only Kansas City had a higher percentage of black residents in its total population, for Negroes constituted 9.43 percent of Indianapolis citizens.[52] The city's whites viewed the increase with dismay and felt the city was deteriorating because of the black influx. In 1910, one local historian lamented that "many objectionable negroes have come here, especially since the southern states began driving out their undesirable classes."[53]

Table 2

Negro Population of Indianapolis 1890-1930

Date	Total Population	Negro Population	Percent Negro
1890	105,436	9,154	7.69
1900	169,164	15,963	9.43
1910	233,650	21,816	9.36
1920	314,194	34,678	11.02
1930	364,161	43,967	12.05

SOURCE: *U.S. Census Reports*, 1890-1930.

Only minimal interaction between the races occurred before 1900, and on the surface little overt indication of racial hostility existed. Avoidance of such tension was more the result of the circumspect behavior of the Negroes than of restraint or tolerance by whites. Such black statements as one acknowledging that "we have learned to forego some rights that are common and because we know the price" caused Emma Lou Thornbrough to observe that "friction was avoided in part by the failure of Negroes to take advantage of all the rights which were legally theirs."[54] The *Freeman*, the main black newspaper for the city, set the tenor for the Negro community with its conservative, conciliatory position. George L. Knox, who became editor of the newspaper in 1897, was a former slave who escaped to the Union forces during the Civil War.[55] Knox was a long-time proponent of Booker T. Washington's ideas, and the newspaper preached his philosophy for years after the black leader's death.

White reaction to Negroes at best was indifferent and in many cases became increasingly hostile as more Negroes settled in Indianapolis. In the early 1900s, Ray Stannard Baker observed during his visit in the Hoosier city that while a few of the Civil War generation maintained their concern for the Negro, most citizens neither knew nor cared about blacks. He found that the only people concerned with the Negro community were a small number of minor politicians, charity workers, and the police.[56] When he talked to other citizens who were aware of the Negro, they generally held a negative view. One complained, "There are too many Negroes up here; they hurt the city." Another white resident declared, "I suppose sooner or later we shall have to adopt some of the restrictions of the South."[57]

Indianapolis Negroes were aware of the tenuous peace existing between the two races, and they too were concerned about the growing number of migrants. In 1903, a group of blacks organized the Colored Business Men's League which was primarily concerned with avoiding "a race war" in the city. Their goal was to force undesirable Negro migrants to leave the city.[58] The *Freeman* warned the following year that untoward action by blacks might not prompt a mob to assemble, but white reaction would manifest itself in other undesirable ways. Therefore, the paper advised the long-time residents and "those that cast their lots with us to be as circumspect as possible, because it is right and it is best."[59]

Negroes in the city were therefore restricted not only by the threat of white hostility but also by their own pragmatic accommodationist stance. For despite their numbers, Indianapolis blacks had virtually no power or influence. Particularly after 1900, Negroes were ignored by Republicans, despite their support for the party.[60] In the 1890s, the Republican county chairman purportedly stated that Negroes were detrimental to the party because they alienated white voters.[61] Few blacks held political appointments throughout the period, and the possibility of placing one of their brothers in a policy-making position on a municipal board was considered unattainable.

Elite reform groups which implemented municipal reform, such as reorganization of the school board, neither sought nor gained involvement from the black community. By 1899, the board of school commissioners was reduced to four elected members and removed from political influence, but the goal of electing a black member was never taken up by Negro citizens because of their lack of power.

Negroes not only were out of the political mainstream, but also were removed from the swelling industrial current. Ray Stannard Baker interviewed numerous Negroes in Indianapolis around 1900 and concluded that their chief complaint was lack of job opportunity and employment discrimination.[62] Virtually no Indianapolis industries would hire Negroes in the early years of the century. Almost all of the city's blacks were relegated to areas of domestic service. The only mitigating factor in the labor scene was the availability of a few more unskilled jobs in Indianapolis than in other northern cities because fewer European immigrants settled there, thus providing a smaller unskilled labor pool. Only 17,122 immigrants resided in the city in 1900.[63] A small number of Negroes were streetcar employees, an unusual area of black job opportunity because only two other cities in the North employed Negroes in this field.[64] Although some opportunity existed in such fields as catering and barbering, in Indianapolis as in other cities whites came to dominate these areas. By 1930, blacks had made few inroads in industry as skilled workers: 76.4 percent of Negro men were employed as unskilled workers, and 83 percent of black women wage earners fell in the same employment category.[65]

At the top of the social and economic hierarchy stood a small number of black doctors, lawyers, and ministers. A larger professional group with similar prestige in the community was the black public school teacher, who constituted 10 percent of the elementary teaching force in the quasi-segregated system. In 1909, sixty-five black teachers taught in the elementary schools designated for their race.[66] It is perhaps because of this important source of employment in the schools that many blacks looked with favor on the school system in the early twentieth century. In 1909, the *Freeman* hailed the board of school commissioners for "the great advance in the colored schools of Indianapolis" in the preceding years.[67] Yet, even then, muted rumblings arose from the white community on the question of a separate black high school. School commissioners and candidates for the board assured the black public that no separate high school was appropriate at that time. Simultaneously, however, the superintendent of schools was informing the school commissioners of the desirability of ultimate segregation in the upper grades.[68]

The delicate peace between the races was shattered in the post-World War I years as more and more Negroes settled in the city. The vast numbers migrating during the war period and the 1920s contributed to the doubling of the black population in a twenty-year period. In 1910, 21,816 Negroes resided there; by 1930, the number had risen to 43,967, or 12 percent of the city's population.[69] Not only the numbers but also the origins of the newcomers disturbed white residents, although Indianapolis had a far higher percentage of Negroes born in Indiana or the two border states, Kentucky and Tennessee, than in the Deep South.[70] Both Kentucky and Tennessee had illiteracy rates among Negroes of slightly over 27 percent.[71] The educational background of students migrating from these border states was so inferior, however, that one study in 1924 established that black children from this region were responsible for the high retardation rate in the Negro schools of Indianapolis.[72]

White indifference or muted opposition was transformed into active hostility toward Negroes in the 1920s, and housing and schools became the battleground. As middle-class Negroes attempted to escape the black enclaves just northwest of the downtown area which were becoming congested as a result of the new settlers, they encountered violent opposition by white property owners. White residents of neighborhoods which blacks attempted to move into retaliated with spite fences, hand grenades, homeowners' leagues, inflammatory handbills, and, in 1926, a blatantly discriminatory housing ordinance. The city council passed a law proclaiming that, "in the interest of public peace, good order and the general welfare, it is advisable to foster the separation of white and negro residential communities." The ordinance declared it illegal for Negroes to reside in a white area or for whites to live in a Negro community unless there was a written consent by a majority of residents living in the neighborhood.[73] The courts ruled the ordinance illegal only after the national office and the local branch of the NAACP collected five thousand dollars and tested the legality of the law.[74]

The conditions existed in the 1920s, therefore, for Indianapolis to gain the dubious reputation as "the center of Klandom."[75] The white Anglo-Saxon Protestant outlook of the city became magnified into the demagogic terrorist "One Hundred Percent Americanism" of the 1920s. David C. Stephenson, Grand Dragon of Indiana, made Indianapolis his headquarters, and by 1924, the Ku Klux Klan boasted a local membership of 40,000.[76] The Invisible Empire drew to its ranks some civic leaders, including the president of one of the banks, but most of the upper class rejected membership in the primarily middle- and lower middle-class organization.[77] To many who refused to join the Klan, however, the exaltation of One Hundred Percent Americanism and racism was attractive. They agreed that the enemy was already within the city, despite the low profile of the black population and the small percentage of immigrants. To many Indianapolis whites, all that was good about the city derived from its WASP qualities. Two local historians in the 1920s pointed with pride to the high percentage of church affiliation among the population and explained that it was attributable to the city's large native-born population, "an extraordinary condition, considering the lax immigration laws of the past decade."[78] A number of ministers in the fundamentalist Protestant churches which dominated Indianapolis religious life chose to take up the fiery cross and preach the Klan's message. One Baptist minister entitled one of his sermons "The Reason for the Existence of the Fiery Cross," and the Brightwood Congregational Church was labeled "the center of Klandom."[79] Other ministers took strong stands against the Invisible Empire. Even ministers opposing the Klan, however, did not indict the prejudices which had traditionally characterized Indianapolis's race relations.

Non-Klan groups such as the chamber of commerce and leading women's organizations supported efforts for further segregation in the city. The Mapleton Civic Association pledged its upper middle-class members not to sell or lease homes to Negroes and to work for total segregation in the schools—measures they proclaimed would make Indianapolis "a better place to live."[80]

By 1924, the Klan was victorious at the polls: Indiana elected a Klan-

dominated governor and state legislature. The Invisible Empire celebrated
its victories by holding a "monster parade" which ominously threaded
its way through the main black section of the city.[81] Further victories
followed in 1925 at the local level, despite a sex scandal and sensational
trial involving Stephenson. The election swept into power a Klan-supported
mayor and school board, even though the *Indianapolis Star* as well as some
civic organizations had begun to wage battle against the scandal-tainted
organization.

By 1928, the Klan era had ended with the Invisible Empire ravaged by
revelations of corruption and torn by division. The racism for which the
Klan stood, however, remained. The organization had manifested a more
violent form of a prejudice embraced by a majority of Indianapolis whites.
Thus, a new community "peace" between the races existed by 1930, a
peace even more oppressive than the one at the turn of the century.
Indianapolis could not make itself a lily white city, but it did succeed in
proscribing mixing of its black and white citizens in nearly every area of
public contact.

CHICAGO

By the end of the nineteenth century, Chicago was an industrial power-
house, providing a home and employment for 1,099,850 urban dwellers.
Immigrants and sons and daughters of immigrants poured into the young
city of promise and by 1890 constituted 77.9 percent of the polyglot
city's population.[82] Negroes, a small ethnic group with a long history in
Chicago, were increasing proportionately even faster than the other groups
(see Table 3). By 1890, over 14,000 Chicagoans, or 1.3 percent of the
city's residents, were black. In the following ten years, the black community doubled, reaching 30,150 in 1900, or 1.9 percent of the 1,698,575
residents of the Windy City. Between 1910 and 1920, the Negro population
exploded from 44,103 to 109,458, representing 4.1 percent of the total
population. In the following ten years, it surged to 233,903, or 6.9 percent
of the 1930 total population of 3,376,438.[83] The metropolis attracted
blacks from many areas of the nation, but from World War I onward, an
increasing number of migrants were making the long journey from the
Deep South. In 1930, over 42 percent of black Chicagoans had their origins
in the red clay of Georgia and Alabama and the black loam of Mississippi
and Louisiana.[84] These Negroes were from the poorest areas of the South.

Table 3

Negro Population of Chicago 1890-1930

Date	Total Population	Negro Population	Percent Negro
1890	1,099,850	14,271	1.3
1900	1,698,575	30,150	1.9
1910	2,185,283	44,103	2.0
1920	2,701,705	109,458	4.1
1930	3,376,438	233,903	6.9

SOURCE: *U.S. Census Reports,* 1890-1930.

Black education was so inferior in the Deep South that in 1910 the illiteracy level among Negroes ranged from 35.6 percent in Mississippi to 48.4 percent in Louisiana.[85]

Residential restrictions forced blacks migrating to the city to settle in the congested South Side, the area St. Clair Drake and Horace Cayton termed the "Black Metropolis."[86] In tracing the rise of this ghetto, Allan Spear observed that, despite the concentration of blacks in the South Side at the end of the nineteenth century, substantial interspersion of blacks and whites existed. Few blocks could be termed strictly Negro blocks.[87] The continual increase of Negroes ended this type of residential integration, and by 1915, the Black Belt had emerged. Almost all Negroes were concentrated within a thin strip south of the business center and in a similar narrow ghetto to the west.

The racial solidarity in part produced by this residential concentration was envied by other black communities. Yet, according to Spear's study, it was neither the result of choice nor necessarily indicative of racial advancement.[88] He contended that Chicago blacks were forced to band together "because a systematic pattern of discrimination left them no alternative."[89] Unlike other ethnic groups which formed enclaves in Chicago by choice, "Negroes were tied together less by a common cultural heritage than by a common set of grievances."[90]

The common set of grievances resulted from the rising white hostility and increased discrimination in the city as blacks became more numerous and conspicuous. White restrictions and the burgeoning physical ghetto also produced a new type of black leadership in the early years of the twentieth century. By 1920, this leadership had "built a complex of community organizations, institutions, and enterprises that made the South Side not simply an area of Negro concentration but a city within a city."[91] Those leaders instrumental in this development were businessmen, professionals, and a new type of politician who depended on the Negro community for their livelihood.[92] While they promoted the development of separate black businesses and racial unity, they also emphasized racial pride and increased political power. Leaders included such activists as Ferdinand and Ida Barnett, politician Edward Wright, and Robert Abbott, editor of the fiery *Chicago Defender*. This newspaper played a vital role in the black community, for it not only reflected the developing racial solidarity and pride on the South Side but also was instrumental in encouraging the growth of the spirit. Furthermore, it served as one of the chief institutions in stimulating the Great Migration. Between 1916 and 1918, the newspaper increased its circulation tenfold as its message of southern oppression and northern opportunity for the Negro pierced deep into the South.[93]

Both the migrant and the long-time black resident were the targets of white resentment. Polish and Irish Chicagoans just west of the Black Belt viewed Negroes as competition on the labor market and potential interlopers in their residential areas. White gangs roamed the Irish and Polish enclaves to see that no blacks made the mistake of crossing Wentworth Avenue, the dividing line between the white and black communities. Middle-class whites living south of the Black Belt were equally hostile. They saw the growing black population as an inferior group in Chicago which threatened to spill over into their neighborhoods and attend their schools.

Religious groups did little to stem the rising tension between the races. One historian wrote that white churches "generally fled in panic before the influx of migrants."[94] In 1918, for example, the black Olivet Baptist congregation was able to buy the First Baptist Church's building because the white group chose to move rather than accept more than miniscule integration.[95]

Some of the city's reformers were more sympathetic toward the Negro, but they were involved primarily in attacking other problems and aiding other groups. Settlement workers and civic leaders recognized that Chicago's mercurial physical and economic growth had come at a high social price. Squalid tenements, industrial conflict, racial prejudice, and political corruption were part of the cost. Prominent Chicagoans surveying their city were appalled, and such men and women as Jane Addams, Graham Taylor, and Sophonisba P. Breckinridge, as well as members of the Civic Federation, mounted an effort to provide needed assistance to immigrants, eliminate graft in city hall, and improve municipal services. Negroes received the attention of only a few reformers in the early twentieth century. For example, in 1904, Celia Parker Wooley established a settlement house for Negroes, the Frederick Douglass Center.[96] Furthermore, two of Chicago's most formidable progressives, Jane Addams and John Dewey, helped form the NAACP. But the vast majority of Chicago Negroes were untouched by such ameliorative efforts and remained unaided by white reform groups.

The brutal consequences of white prejudice and discrimination received public attention and careful documentation only after the 1919 riot. The official report of the Chicago Commission on Race Relations, *The Negro in Chicago,* proclaimed: "Negroes in Illinois are legally entitled to all the rights and privileges of other citizens. Actually, however, their participation in public benefits in practically every field is limited by some circumvention of the law."[97] The report cited housing as a critical area of discrimination and conflict. Not only were few apartments, houses, or rooms available for Negroes, but also those which were open to them were substandard, overpriced, and crowded. Housing costs for unheated flats for native whites in Chicago averaged from twenty to twenty-five dollars per month, while for Negroes rent for the same type of flat averaged from twenty-five to thirty dollars.[98] One study in 1909 by the Chicago School of Civics and Philanthropy compared Negro housing districts with those of other low-income groups. Seventy-one percent of the houses in a Polish district, 57 percent in a Bohemian district, and 54 percent in the stockyards were in good repair, and only 26 percent in the Negro district.[99]

The quest for adequate housing by Negroes crushed in the overcrowded Black Belt produced bitter block-by-block opposition by whites who feared loss of property values. Restrictive housing covenants, harassment, and bombings of black homes increased during the war years, and the growing white hostility contributed to the explosive situation which was responsible for the bloody riot in 1919 that left 38 dead and 537 injured.[100]

Blacks in industry and business also experienced discrimination. Before

World War I, the multitude of industries which polluted the midwestern skies put immigrants to work as quickly as they arrived, but they frequently rejected black workers—except as strike breakers. Over 65 percent of the black men and over 80 percent of the Negro women were in domestic and personal service fields in 1900. Manufacturing engaged only 8.3 percent of the men and 11.9 percent of the women. Ten years later, the employment patterns were almost the same. More than 45 percent of employed Negro men in 1910 worked in four fields—as servants, waiters, porters, and janitors.[101] Even during the flush days of World War I when Negro employment in industry surged upward, businesses such as traction companies, department stores, and taxicab companies remained closed to blacks.[102]

In analyzing the volatile issues of housing, employment, and crime, the commission continually returned to public opinion as the greatest source of racial discord and discrimination in the city. They cited the influence of the white press as critical in molding public opinion. Analysis of the racial policies of the three leading white newspapers convinced the commission that misrepresentation of Negroes and emphasis on black crime and Negro "invasion" of white neighborhoods heightened and reinforced public prejudice.[103]

Inferior recreation centers, inadequate sanitation facilities, discrimination in places of public accommodation—these were also the lot of the Chicago Negro. The large black community was not helpless, however. Its members had potential power in their numbers, and in some areas they made more significant advances than any other black community in the nation. Politically, Chicago blacks scored a number of notable victories. Before 1914, only one Chicago Negro served in the state legislature, whereas the number rose to two in 1914, three in 1918, four in 1924, and five in 1928. At the local level, they elected a black alderman in 1915 and another in 1918. Finally, in 1928, they sent the first Negro to Congress since Reconstruction.[104]

Negroes represented a solid bloc of Republican votes, and this power brought deference from local politicians such as the formidable William Hale Thompson, Chicago's controversial mayor from 1915 to 1923 and 1927 to 1931. Power also bought jobs from the Republican machine. In 1932, Harold Gosnell estimated that 6.4 percent of the employees on the city payroll were black.[105] This figure was almost equivalent to the percentage of blacks in the total population. The jobs ranged from janitor to assistant state's attorney, with 400 of the black employees listed in the clerical, professional, or administrative areas and 1,468 in the categories of janitors, laborers, or temporary help.[106]

Despite the number of jobs which the machine offered the black community, machine politics proved to be undeserving of unqualified black support. Condemnation of Chicago's political system was apparent in the Race Commission report; however, both blacks and whites failed to recognize it.[107]

Some indication of the failure of the touted Chicago black political power and the related machine system is evident in Harold F. Gosnell's *Negro Politicians,* published in 1935. The political scientist observed that in the thirteen years since the Race Commission made its recommendations, politicians' records related to Negroes were at best mixed. He acknowledged that residential bombings aimed at Negroes had decreased and that no further riots had rocked the city. But he charged that "Negro politicians have been unable or unwilling to prevent police brutality, to check crime conditions in the Negro community, to insist upon adequate recreational and educational facilities, to provide the best possible health services, and to secure sufficient housing at reasonable rentals."[108] It is unlikely that any local government or group of politicians could have succeeded in all of these areas. As James Q. Wilson observed, "No matter who controlled it, city hall in the 1930's did not have the power to change substantially the life chances of many Negroes—or of anyone else, for that matter."[109] But Wilson and Gosnell did argue that more could have been achieved and that Negro politicians were partly to blame—especially in the areas of law enforcement and public education.[110] Black politicians refused to support investigation of city and school board finances and policies, rejected the anti-injunction bill and the eight-hour law for women, and opposed the extension of the civil service system.[111] Thus, some observers claimed that the political power of Chicago Negroes had been wasted— they had "sold their birthright for a mess of gambling privileges and petty jobs."[112]

One of the white power bastions which black power was unable to scale was the board of education, despite the political nature of the selection of board members. In 1891, the state legislature passed a law providing for a twenty-one member board of education in Chicago. The mayor was empowered to appoint the members of the board with the advice and consent of the common council.[113] In 1917, the board was reduced to eleven members who were appointed in the same way. George

Counts condemned the consequences of the procedure in *School and Society in Chicago,* citing the corruption which had marred the board's actions. The appointment method, he declared, "bound the school system to the city hall and has subordinated the interests of education to the vagaries and vicissitudes of partisan politics." He characterized the board members as "creatures of the mayor" who "must either do his bidding or resign."[114]

Counts' analysis of the composition of the board over a twenty-year period revealed its exclusive nature, a characteristic which prevailed among the educational policy-makers of all three cities and which made Negroes protest their lack of representation. He described the members as drawn almost entirely from "the middle and favored classes."[115] Not even during the administrations of William Thompson, the man labeled by black Chicagoans as "the second Lincoln," did Negroes succeed in placing a spokesman for black citizens on the board.

Despite the constant influx of migrants and the wide variation in social status and background, the Chicago Negro community was a more cohesive group than either Indianapolis's or Philadelphia's. Chicago's militant black leadership, the concentration of Negroes in one area of the city, and the political activism of blacks all contributed to this unity. Although Chicago's ghetto had spawned a number of black businesses and professionals, the community still lacked a substantial middle class. According to James Q. Wilson, this small middle class could not provide "the kind of infrastructure necessary to support either a significant protest movement or to constitute a base of power outside the political apparatus."[116]

Chicago blacks were proud of their city's image as a black haven and a center of Negro political power, but they were keenly aware of their limitations as a group and of the paradoxical nature of Chicago. The economic, educational, and social opportunity there was far greater than that which southern society or many other northern cities offered. Yet, it was a city where racial tension had increased as the black population rose, finally bursting into the terror of a week-long race riot in 1919. Even in its aftermath, as whites and blacks sought the reasons for the prejudice and injustice, entrenched discrimination and limitations hobbled black Chicago in the realization of economic security and social equality.

Thus, the three black communities were plagued by numerous common problems. In each of the cities, blacks confronted economic and social institutions committed to keeping the Negro in an inferior position. This lack of economic opportunity meant that in no city was the black middle or upper class large enough to provide effective pressure groups and a significant number of individuals with the time and influence to work successfully for racial justice.

In none of the cities did increased numbers produce substantive racial advancement. In Chicago, the black population's growth brought greater political power, but in no other area in the Windy City nor in the other two were blacks able to realize real social or economic gains in the first thirty years of this century. In fact, the migration unleashed waves of racism which increased residential segregation, produced more racially separate schools, and escalated racial conflict.

Yet, differences existed among the cities. Three different philosophies of racial advancement were represented in the cities. In Indianapolis until the mid-1920s, the strategy of Booker T. Washington dominated the black community and produced an accommodationist stance of self-help, support of separate schools staffed by black teachers, and eschewal of political or judicial action as tools of racial progress. This conservative philosophy was in part dictated by the virulent prejudice and tactics of the white community.

In Philadelphia, the black community was unified neither geographically nor philosophically. Philadelphia Negroes were divided between advocating integrated facilities, especially schools, and accepting segregated facilities which offered more job opportunities. They were also at odds over strategy. Should blacks turn to court action and militant responses such as school boycotts, or should they rely on low-keyed consultations between black and white leaders? No satisfactory answer emerged in this period. The political situation in the city hindered black political power because the city was dominated by the Republican machine which had little need to actively woo black voters or provide black supporters with a substantial number of political jobs. Job opportunities were also affected by the separation of the black community into three enclaves which could not support many black businessmen or professionals.

While the black community in Philadelphia displayed a comparatively nonmilitant stance devoid of great shows of racial unity or power, the white community exhibited a similar lack of dramatic opposition. No major riots or firebombs punctuated white actions toward blacks. Nevertheless, prejudice and segregationist policies manifested themselves in more subtle but highly effective ways.

Chicago blacks, in contrast, experienced violent displays of white prejudice through bombings, gang attacks, and a riot. Yet, Chicago Negroes responded with strong racial unity and militant opposition which were in marked contrast to the positions of Philadelphia or Indianapolis blacks. Chicago Negroes gained part of their unity and decisiveness from their political situation. They lived in a city where every political election was close and where Negro votes were vital to a Republican victory. They were therefore able to gain political leverage and municipal jobs. The great Black Belt, although emerging in response to white prejudice, also supported more black businessmen and professionals who could offer leadership for racial causes. Therefore, separate schools for the sake of additional jobs for blacks had less appeal to this community.

The differing conditions and philosophies of the three cities did not, however, protect any age group or economic class in these black communities from experiencing limited opportunities and white hostility. The black child did not go unscarred by these conditions, and the following chapter suggests how this hostile environment affected the Negro child.

NOTES

1. Jacque Voegeli, *Free But Not Equal* (Chicago: University of Chicago Press, 1967), p. 177.

2. Leon F. Litwack, *North of Slavery: The Negro in the Free States, 1790-1860* (Chicago: University of Chicago Press, 1961), p. 279.

3. Forrest G. Wood, *Black Scare: The Racist Response to Emancipation and Reconstruction* (Berkeley: University of California Press, 1968), Ch. 1.

4. Stanley P. Hirshon, *Farewell to the Bloody Shirt: Northern Republicans and the Southern Negro, 1877-1893* (Bloomington: Indiana University Press, 1962), p. 18.

5. W.E.B. DuBois, *The Philadelphia Negro*, University of Pennsylvania Series in Political Economy and Public Law, No. 14 (Philadelphia: University of Pennsylvania, 1899), p. 33.

6. Stanley Lieberson, *Ethnic Patterns in American Cities* (New York: Free Press of Glencoe, 1963), p. 122.

7. Sadie T. Mossell, "The Standard of Living Among One Hundred Negro Migrant Families in Philadelphia," *Annals of the American Academy of Political and Social Science* 98 (November 1921): 177.

8. See Sterling D. Spero and Abram L. Harris, *The Black Worker* (New York: Columbia University Press, 1931), p. 12, for a discussion of the labor rivalry aspect of Philadelphia racial tension. For a good analysis of the urban experience of blacks in nineteenth-century Philadelphia, see Theodore Hershberg, "Free Blacks in Ante-

bellum Philadelphia: A Study of Ex-Slaves, Freeborn, and Socio-economic Decline," *Journal of Social History* 4 (Summer 1971): 333-356.

9. Sam Bass Warner, Jr., *The Private City* (Philadelphia: University of Pennsylvania Press, 1968), p. 126.

10. DuBois, *Philadelphia Negro*, p. 43.

11. *U.S. Eleventh Census*, 1890, Vol. 1, *Population*, pp. 449, 731.

12. Note that the class structure of black northern communities was such that most of the members of the black upper class would probably not have qualified as upper class in the white community but as members of the middle class. See August Meier, *Negro Thought in America 1880-1915* (Ann Arbor: University of Michigan Press, 1963), pp. 149-157.

13. DuBois, *Philadelphia Negro*, p. 317.

14. *Philadelphia Tribune*, March 5, 1927.

15. *U.S. Fifteenth Census*, 1930, Vol. 4, *Population*, pp. 448-450, 505-506, 1414-1415.

16. H. Viscount Nelson, Jr., "Race and Class Consciousness of Philadelphia Negroes with Special Emphasis on the Years Between 1927 and 1940" (Ph.D. dissertation, University of Pennsylvania, 1969), p. 14.

17. *U.S. Twelfth Census*, 1900, Vol. 1, *Population*, part 1, p. cxxi; *U.S. Thirteenth Census*, 1910, Vol. 1, *Population*, part 1, p. 211; *U.S. Fourteenth Census*, 1920, Vol. 2, *Population*, p. 47; *Abstract of the Fifteenth Census of the U.S.*, 1930, p. 98.

18. U.S. Bureau of the Census, *Negro Population in the United States, 1790-1915* (Washington, D.C.: U.S. Government Printing Office, 1918), pp. 75-79, 428. (See Chapter 2 for a discussion of the educational conditions of Negroes in the South.)

19. Commonwealth of Pennsylvania, Department of Welfare, *Negro Survey of Pennsylvania* (Harrisburg, Pa.: Department of Welfare, 1927), p. 85.

20. Mossell, "Standard of Living," p. 177.

21. Clara A. Hardin, *The Negroes of Philadelphia: The Cultural Adjustment of a Minority Group* (Bryn Mawr, Pa.: By the Author, 1945), p. iii.

22. *Philadelphia Tribune*, March 12, 1927.

23. James Erroll Miller, "The Negro in Pennsylvania Politics with Special Reference to Philadelphia Since 1932" (Ph.D. dissertation, University of Pennsylvania, 1945), p. 123.

24. W.E.B. DuBois, "The Black Vote of Philadelphia," *Charities* 15 (October 7, 1905): 34.

25. DuBois, *Philadelphia Negro*, p. 384.

26. *Philadelphia Tribune*, February 15, 1913; January 3, 1914.

27. See William Henry Issel, "Schools for a Modern Age: Educational Reform in Pennsylvania in the Progressive Era" (Ph.D. dissertation, University of Pennsylvania, 1969), pp. 268-269, for a discussion of this characteristic "reform by imposition."

28. DuBois, *Philadelphia Negro*, pp. 383-384.

29. Philadelphia Public Education Association, *A Generation of Progress in*

Our Public Schools, 1881-1912 (Philadelphia: Public Education Association of Philadelphia, 1914), p. 5.

30. Hazel C. MacLean, "Evolution of the Philadelphia School System Since the Year 1818" (M.A. thesis, Temple University, 1930), p. 87. For a similar trend in municipal government reform, see Samuel P. Hays, "The Politics of Reform in Municipal Government in the Progressive Era," *Pacific Northwest Quarterly* 55 (October 1964): 157-169.

31. MacLean, "Evolution of the Philadelphia School System," p. 87.

32. DuBois, *Philadelphia Negro,* p. 109.

33. Commonwealth of Pennsylvania, *Negro Survey of Pennsylvania,* p. 20.

34. DuBois, *Philadelphia Negro,* p. 337.

35. Spero and Harris, *The Black Worker,* p. 60.

36. Commonwealth of Pennsylvania, *Negro Survey of Pennsylvania,* p. 20.

37. Simpson, *Negro in the Philadelphia Press,* p. 109.

38. Commonwealth of Pennsylvania, *Negro Survey of Pennsylvania,* p. 53.

39. Ibid., p. 56.

40. Mossell, "Standard of Living," p. 217.

41. *Philadelphia Public Ledger,* July 29, 1918.

42. Lieberson, *Ethnic Patterns in American Cities,* p. 122.

43. John T. Gillard, *The Catholic Church and the American Negro* (Baltimore: St. Joseph's Society Press, 1929), p. 126.

44. Mossell, "Standard of Living," p. 177.

45. Simpson, *Negro in the Philadelphia Press,* p. 177.

46. Ibid., p. 115.

47. Ibid., p. 116.

48. Detweiler, *Negro Press in the United States,* pp. 53-54.

49. Emma Lou Thornbrough, *The Negro in Indiana Before 1900* (Indianapolis: Indiana Historical Bureau, 1957), pp. 55-91.

50. U.S. Bureau of the Census, *Negroes in the United States,* Bulletin 8 (1904): 102.

51. *U.S. Eleventh Census,* 1890, Vol. 1, *Population,* pp. 446, 679; *U.S. Twelfth Census,* Vol. 1, *Population,* part 1, p. cxix.

52. U.S. Bureau of the Census, *Negroes in the United States,* pp. 230-231, 269-271.

53. Jacob Piatt Dunn, *Greater Indianapolis,* Vol. 1 (Chicago: Lewis Publishing Co., 1910), p. 253.

54. Emma Lou Thornbrough, "Segregation in Indiana During the Klan Era of the 1920s," *Mississippi Valley Historical Review* 48 (March 1961): 597.

55. Detweiler, *Negro Press in the United States,* p. 57.

56. Ray Stannard Baker, *Following the Color Line* (New York: Doubleday, Page and Co., 1908), p. 17.

57. Ibid., p. 118.

58. *Indianapolis Freeman,* August 3, 1903.

59. Ibid., September 3, 1904.

60. Dunn, *Greater Indianapolis,* Vol. 1, p. 253.

61. Thornbrough, *Negro in Indiana,* p. 308.

62. Baker, *Following the Color Line,* p. 131.

63. Thornbrough, *Negro in Indiana,* pp. 350-351.

64. James S. Stemons, "The Industrial Color-Line in the North," *Century Illustrated Magazine* 60 (July 1900): 478.

65. Flanner House, *The Indianapolis Story* (Indianapolis: n.p., 1939), p. 14.

66. Dunn, *Greater Indianapolis,* Vol. 1, p. 280.

67. *Indianapolis Freeman,* October 23, 1909.

68. Ibid., October 30, 1909; Indianapolis Board of School Commissioners, *Minutes,* Book 0, October 29, 1907, p. 77.

69. *U.S. Thirteenth Census,* 1910, Vol. 1, *Population,* part 1, p. 209; *Abstract of the Fifteenth Census of the U.S.,* 1930, p. 98.

70. U.S. Bureau of the Census, *Negroes in the United States, 1920-1932* (Washington, D.C.: U.S. Government Printing Office, 1935), p. 349.

71. U.S. Bureau of the Census, *Negro Population in the United States,* p. 420.

72. Julian Dorster Coleman, "Are Out of Town Children Responsible for the Retardation in the Colored Schools of Indianapolis, Indiana?" (M.A. thesis, University of Chicago, 1924), pp. 80-84.

73. *Journal of the Common Council of the City of Indianapolis, Indiana,* from January 1, 1926, to December 1, 1926 (Indianapolis: City of Indianapolis, 1927), p. 54.

74. Thornbrough, "Segregation in Indiana," p. 600.

75. See Kenneth T. Jackson, *The Ku Klux Klan in the City, 1915-1930* (New York: Oxford University Press, 1967), Ch. 10.

76. Ibid., p. 154.

77. Ibid., p. 145.

78. Kate Milner Rabb and William Herschell, eds., *An Account of Indianapolis and Marion County,* Vol. 3 of *History of Indiana,* ed. by Logan Esarey (Dayton, Ohio: Dayton Historical Publishing Co., 1924), p. 151.

79. Jackson, *Ku Klux Klan in the City,* p. 150.

80. *Indianapolis Freeman,* March 1, 1924.

81. Jackson, *Ku Klux Klan in the City,* p. 156.

82. Bessie Louise Pierce, *History of Chicago,* Vol. 3 (New York: Alfred A. Knopf, 1957), p. 22.

83. *U.S. Eleventh Census,* 1890, Vol. 1, *Population,* p. 443; *U.S. Twelfth Census,* 1900, Vol. 1, *Population,* part 1, p. cxxi; *U.S. Thirteenth Census,* 1910, Vol. 1, *Population,* part 1, p. 211; *U.S. Fourteenth Census,* 1920, Vol. 2, *Population,* p. 43; *Abstract of the Fifteenth Census of the U.S.,* 1930, p. 98.

84. U.S. Bureau of the Census, *Negroes in the United States, 1920-1932,* pp. 32-36.

85. U.S. Bureau of the Census, *Negro Population in the United States,* p. 428.

86. St. Clair Drake and Horace Cayton, *Black Metropolis* (New York: Harcourt, Brace and Co., 1945).

87. Allan H. Spear, *Black Chicago: The Making of a Negro Ghetto, 1890-1920* (Chicago: University of Chicago Press, 1967), p. 11.

88. Ibid., p. 225.

89. Ibid., p. 228

90. Ibid.

91. Ibid., p. 91.

92. Ibid., Ch. 5.

93. William M. Tuttle, Jr., *Race Riot: Chicago in the Red Summer of 1919* (New York: Atheneum, 1972), pp. 89-90.

94. Ibid., p. 98.

95. Ibid.

96. Allen F. Davis, *Spearheads for Reform* (New York: Oxford University Press, 1967), p. 95.

97. Chicago Commission on Race Relations, *The Negro in Chicago: A Study of Race Relations and a Race Riot* (Chicago: University of Chicago Press, 1922), p. 614.

98. Jennie D. Porter, "Problems of Negro Education in Northern and Border Cities" (Ph.D. dissertation, University of Cincinnati, 1928), p. 99.

99. Alzada P. Comstock, "Chicago Housing Conditions, VI: The Problem of the Negro," *American Journal of Sociology* (Chicago), 18 (September 1912): 244-245.

100. See William Tuttle's detailed analysis of the riot and its causes in *Race Riot*.

101. Spear, *Black Chicago*, p. 29.

102. Chicago Commission on Race Relations, *Negro in Chicago*, pp. 391-392.

103. Ibid., pp. 634-636.

104. James Q. Wilson in Harold F. Gosnell, *Negro Politicians*, 2nd ed. (Chicago: University of Chicago Press, 1967), p. viii.

105. Gosnell, *Negro Politicians*, p. 239.

106. Ibid.

107. Ibid., p. 370.

108. Ibid., p. 371.

109. Ibid., p. xi.

110. Ibid.

111. Ibid.

112. Ibid., p. 371.

113. George S. Counts, *School and Society in Chicago* (New York: Harcourt, Brace and Co., 1928), p. 36.

114. Ibid., p. 39.

115. Ibid., p. 49.

116. Wilson in Gosnell, *Negro Politicians*, p. vi.

2 OUTSIDE THE CLASSROOM: THE ENVIRONMENT OF THE BLACK CHILD

The culturally deprived child who dominated the agonized exposes of educational reformers in the 1960s was not a newly discovered victim of the ghettos, just as the ghettos themselves had long been an enclave of victims of urbanization. Educators and social workers in the early part of the century had reported unemployment in Chicago, alley shanties in Indianapolis, and an inordinate death rate among Philadelphia Negroes. The implications of these conditions which plagued almost all blacks living in metropolitan areas did not escape people concerned about black school-children. In 1913, Francis Blascoer made the first full-length study of the ramifications of these dreary statistics on a Negro child's life within the school as well as within the larger community.[1] Negroes themselves grieved over the environmental problems which hindered their children in the schools. "Too many of our children of school age are deprived of good healthy home influence," lamented a Philadelphia Negro newspaper in 1912. "Too many are forced to leave their home without partaking of a breakfast prepared by a loving mother."[2]

Yet, then as now, the concept of the culturally deprived child served as a two-edged sword in educational policy and thought. It slashed and pierced some of the racist assumptions of Negro inferiority based on the level of achievement of black students. It also frequently impaled the children by freeing the educational system from responsibility for the failure of the schools with these students.

Recent historical investigations have pushed the date of the emergence of the black ghettos far back before World War I. The early twentieth-century ghetto was characterized by many of the same depressing characteristics which fill the pages of race commission reports today. If contemporary historians are correct that education has successfully served only those groups which have already achieved a certain degree of economic stability and potential mobility, then the economic conditions of northern Negroes must be considered as a critical factor in understanding the Negro experience in the schools.[3] As suggested in Chapter 1, the Negro found little opportunity for employment within northern industry until the outbreak of World War I. Migrant as well as native blacks were restricted almost exclusively to personal and domestic service fields. Kelly Miller protested in 1906 that "the Negro [in northern states] is compelled to loiter around the edges of industry."[4]

During World War I, Negroes had begun to make inroads in northern industry because of the paucity of cheap immigrant labor. In 1920, the Chicago Race Commission reported that in the preceding five years there had been a decided increase in the number of Negroes in manufacturing, clerical occupations, and laundries.[5] Indianapolis and Philadelphia Negroes experienced similar expansion of opportunity during the war years; however, most of the jobs were for unskilled rather than skilled labor, and throughout the period, inadequate job opportunities were uppermost in most Negroes' minds. In 1928, the Bureau of Child Study of the Chicago Board of Education described the environment of the black child in that city as a world "where unemployment is rife and where every street corner is populated by idle men."[6]

The effect of limited job options on Negro attitudes toward the value of education cannot be overestimated. In Indianapolis, young men who had gone to high school stood idle on the streets. A Negro asked a white reporter, "What shall we do? Here are our young people educated in the schools, capable of doing good work in many occupations where skill and intelligence are required—and yet with few opportunities opening for them." He continued, "They don't want to dig ditches or become porters or valets any more than intelligent white boys."[7]

While black Americans often despaired about the ability of education to open the closed doors to satisfactory employment, many Negroes nevertheless greatly valued the power of education to bring about racial advancement. As Henry J. Perkinson argues in his critique of modern

American education, *The Imperfect Panacea,* Martin Luther King "was the first Negro leader to reject schooling as the panacea for the problem of the Negro."[8] This same faith in education was shown by potential migrants who were lured to the cities by superior northern educational facilities. Letters written to the *Chicago Defender* by southern Negroes reflect their interest in the schools. One parent in Augusta wrote: "My children I wished to be educated in a different community than here. Where the school facilities are better and less prejudice shown. . . ."[9] A young man wrote the *Defender* describing his plans to finish school in the North and requesting "the name of the best high school in Chicago."[10]

Yet, the Negro faith in the power of schooling seemed misplaced in the early part of the century, just as it does now when bleak figures of educational failure emerge from inner city schools. Many Negro students recognized the impotence of education. In 1913, a study of Chicago Negroes described the discouragement young blacks in the city felt about the value of a high school education because of "the tendency of the employers who used colored persons at all in their business to assign them to the most menial labor."[11] Richard Wright, Jr., observed the same attitude among black students in Philadelphia. The four-year course in high school held little appeal to Negroes because "a Negro girl finishing the eighth grade at present, has about as much chance economically as her sister from high school."[12]

An Indianapolis black teacher wrote that it was extremely difficult to motivate Negro students "whose parents daily suffered the grosser aspects of American racism and many of whose brothers and sisters, having completed high school, found themselves unable to find a job commensurate with their education." Yet, "in spite of the bitterness many teachers felt," he recalled that the city's black educators "taught, almost without exception, the great American myth of opportunity for all and 'plenty of room at the top.' "[13]

Studies made during the 1920s indicate that the economic conditions for trained Negroes did not improve substantially. A survey of one hundred black graduates of Wendell Phillips High School in Chicago revealed that many girls who were qualified as typists and stenographers were forced to take unskilled factory jobs. Male graduates complained of similar restrictions.[14] Figures compiled by the Chicago Vocational Guidance Bureau in 1928 indicated that, although there were more Negro children applying for employment than handicapped white children (crippled, paralyzed, etc.), 40.24 percent of the handicapped children gained employment, while only 31.86 percent of the Negro children found jobs.[15]

While job discrimination, with its accompanying effects of low income and curtailed ambition, was a constant difficulty for northern Negroes, black Americans faced other problems in the community which frequently affected the experience of their children in the schools. Housing segregation characterized all northern cities and was a significant factor in the hardening of race relations between the Negro and white community during the period. (The obvious connection between housing restriction and the concomitant de facto segregation in the schools is discussed in later chapters.) Other results of housing discrimination were equally apparent. High rent and inadequate space plagued Negroes in each of the three cities. In Chicago, two- and three-story homes abandoned by white families were divided into multiple apartments and buffet flats, usually without adequate ventilation, light, or sanitation. In Indianapolis, alley homes were the chief type of Negro housing. These structures were "long rows of cheap one-story frame tenements in back streets and alleys which consisted of two or three rooms each."[16] A black doctoral candidate at the University of Pennsylvania investigated Negro housing in Philadelphia in 1919 and made the following notes about some of the conditions she encountered: "Toilet drainage out of repair. . . . Underground leakage that keeps water from the toilet in the yard. . . . So much smoke in the house that I thought it must be on fire." She discovered that garbage facilities were so poor in many cases that tenants used cellars and yards as dumping grounds for their refuse.[17]

The poor sanitary facilities and crowded conditions often made Negro homes breeding grounds of disease. The rate of disease and mortality among Negroes in these cities was always far higher than within the white community. In Philadelphia in the 1890s, DuBois found that the average number of deaths of whites, native-born and immigrant, was 2,269.19 per 100,000 population, while for Negroes it was 3,124.81[18] An Indianapolis doctor reported that the deaths of Negroes from tuberculosis constituted over half the total deaths from the disease in the city, while the black population accounted for only one-eighth of the total.[19] Table 4 indicates that by 1930 mortality rates for Negroes in these three cities were still substantially higher than those for whites.[20]

Table 4

Negro and White Death Rate (Exclusive of Stillbirths) from All Causes for Three Cities: 1930

City and Race	Rate per 1,000 Population
Chicago	
Negro	15.4
White	10.0
Philadelphia	
Negro	16.1
White	12.1
Indianapolis	
Negro	19.6
White	13.5

SOURCE: U.S. Bureau of the Census, *Negroes in the United States, 1920-1932* (Washington, D.C.: U.S. Government Printing Office, 1935), p. 452.

The poor physical condition of Negro students often caused irregular attendance, lethargic attitudes, scholastic retardation, and disciplinary problems. In 1914, one Negro school in Philadelphia introduced a program, the open window class, which had been successful with other lower class children in poor health. The class enrolled children described as "the anemic, the rachitic, the flat and narrow chested . . . almost every variety of the devitalized and poorly nourished."[21] Each had a history of listlessness, inertia, and retardation in his or her classes. Many were exceptional disciplinary problems. After an intensive six-month program of fresh air, hot breakfast, and physical exercise, teachers experienced no disciplinary problems with the children and termed them "alert and interested in their work . . . no longer quarrelsome and irritable."[22]

The low wages and high rent which plagued Negroes contributed to another problem for black families—the necessity of mothers taking jobs away from home. Without supervision, children often overslept, went to school without breakfast, or remained at home to care for younger brothers and sisters. A survey made by principals of Chicago South Side schools with the highest Negro enrollments established that 33.5 percent of the pupils were by themselves "either all or part of the time" because both parents worked.[23] A study of Philadelphia Negro students in 1913 concluded that more than 60 percent of the mothers worked away from home. The survey related this condition to the high rate of absences among the Negro children.[24]

In Philadelphia, the average attendance for five years among the total pupils of the city was 87.7 percent, while for students in Negro schools the average was only 78.8 percent. Furthermore, no Negro schools had as high a percentage of attendance as the average white schools.[25] Indianapolis schools experienced a similar pattern of higher nonattendance in the black schools than in others. After the director of the truancy department for the Indianapolis schools spent several months investigating the conditions which caused the high absentee rate among Negroes, she concluded that the absence of parents from the home due to employment was a chief problem. In the 1909 report, the director of truancy remarked, "Taking into consideration the number of colored children who are deprived of a mother's care during a great part of their childhood, the school attendance, faulty though it be, speaks well for the inclinations of the average colored child."[26]

The problems of truancy and nonattendance among the poorer children in Chicago were so great that in 1917 Edith Abbott and Sophonisba Breckinridge investigated nine elementary schools in the most crowded areas of the city, including two schools with high Negro enrollments. After studying the causes of absence, they became convinced that nonattendance due to responsibilities at home and general conditions of poverty produced far more absences than did truancy. In the vast majority of cases, the two University of Chicago faculty members reported, "it was found that the children were absent with their parents' consent or at their parents' command."[27] Absences among lower-class children were often the result of situations such as one Abbott and Breckinridge reported: A fourteen-year-old girl in the third grade had been absent sixty-two half-days during a six-month period. Investigations found her at home caring for her mother, who had been severely beaten by her father before he deserted the family of five.[28]

Many children were absent for prolonged periods because of lack of clothes, especially shoes. Others would come to school inadequately clad and defensive about their appearance. A letter from a mother to a teacher illustrates this familiar situation in Negro schools:

> Arthur hasn't no clothes to wear. He has on all the clothes he got, and I have not a penny to buy some. He can come to school with his face and hands clean, but his clothes he cannot do any better. I sent him to the county agent for shoes the third time and they won't give him no shoes. . . . The shoes he got on now he found them in the alley.[29]

The temporary nature of the Negroes' jobs ("last hired, first fired" was a familiar concept to all northern blacks) and the constant search for more adequate housing also impeded Negro students. Often they had to adjust to several schools within a single school year. One principal in a school with a black enrollment of 98 percent discovered with dismay that in the preceding year 774 children transferred out of his school and 475 children entered by transfer. Since the total school body was seventeen hundred, only 54 percent of the children enrolled in September remained throughout the school year.[30] In Philadelphia in 1913, Negro students transferred from ward to ward twice as often as did white students.[31]

The number of transfers and the inability of the school system to process the transfers efficiently were serious problems in cities the size of Chicago. One report revealed that Chicago's practice of the old school maintaining responsibility for reporting the absence of a child who failed to enroll in a new school within three days often meant that "transferred children are sometimes lost track of because the transfers are issued to the wrong school."[32]

Not only did these debilitating conditions in the northern cities affect children, but pupils who had migrated from the South bore an additional handicap—an inferior educational background. Children who had begun school in one-room huts, taught by semiliterate teachers for an average of three months per school year, were woefully unprepared for northern school systems. Negro children who migrated from South Carolina around 1915, for example, had attended school for a maximum of sixty-seven days per year.[33] The annual expenditures for Negro students compared with those for white children in states from which many migrants came were in sharp contrast (see Table 5).

Table 5

Per Capita Annual Expenditures for the Education of White and Negro Children in Selected Southern States

States	1914-1915	
	White	Negro
Alabama	9.00	1.47
Georgia	10.09	2.08
Kentucky	10.30	8.91
Louisiana	16.44	1.81
Mississippi	8.20	1.53
North Carolina	7.38	2.66
South Carolina	10.70	1.09
Tennessee	8.70	4.58
Virginia	11.47	3.20

SOURCE: Monroe N. Work, *The Negro Year Book, 1916-17* (Tuskegee Institute, Ala.: The Negro Year Book Publishing Co., 1917).

DuBois investigated the southern Negro common school in 1901 and questioned the teachers about their schools. The replies included such comments as "I have a verry [*sic*] good school at this place. The children are somewhat backwards in their study. I think that is due to the shortness in the school term in this county which are only 16 weeks for the year."[34] Another described the usual facilities: "If you will peep at some dilapidated old barns where the owner had built a new one, you will have some idea of our school houses."[35] One teacher in a medium-sized town remarked that "this county is very destitute of competent teachers" because most "do not possess even a common school education. The reason for this is the pay is so small. . . . They usually get from $5 to $20 per month."[36]

One boy enrolled in a Chicago school had attended school in a small southern country town. He was fifteen years old and six years behind his grade. He explained that one of his teachers had been the town iceman. "He didn't come to school until he was through totin' ice around. Then, if anyone wanted ice they comed after him."[37]

Children coming to the cities with such educational backgrounds were sometimes placed in a regular class. Many cities, including Chicago and Indianapolis, had special ungraded rooms for migrant students.[38] The results of such rooms were mixed. On occasion children who initially appeared quite retarded advanced quickly in ungraded rooms. One Chicago teacher stated that children who were unable to read or write when they arrived improved rapidly and within a year were able to do fourth, fifth, and sixth grade assignments.[39] While these special rooms were frequently criticized as devices for segregating Negro children in mixed schools, they often allowed for more educational advancement than the policy of placing a child in a regular class with students six or seven years younger.

The quality of Negro education and facilities in all areas of the South was inferior to that in the North throughout the period. As late as the early 1930s, a survey of Negro students in a southern state revealed that the children wrote somewhat more slowly than white students. This difference was explained when the tester noticed that "a great many of the children did not have pencils of their own."[40] He also observed that many Negro schools were unable to provide any textbooks for the students.[41]

Experience with large numbers of immigrant children helped educators realize the need for the school to deal with problems and conditions outside the classroom which affected the students' progress. Social workers, however, encountered some educators who had comparatively little appreciation of the close relationship between home conditions and school behavior and progress. Iva Evelyn Smith recorded cases in Chicago where a student's problems produced by home circumstances were ignored or dealt with only by severe disciplinary treatment until the child's behavior became so intolerable to the teacher that the only solution was to transfer the student.[42]

Administrators and social workers, influenced by the Progressive movement, embraced the idea of expanded school services which would reach beyond the school and deal at least superficially with some of the environmental conditions affecting their lower-class clients, especially the foreign born and the black. It cannot be stressed too strongly, however, that the schoolmen themselves believed they had only a limited role in mitigating these problems. As discussed in Chapter 4, the schools did not attempt to deal with the fundamental social discrimination which produced or exacerbated many of the Negro's problems.

Another limiting factor was the attitude of schoolmen and the larger society toward the detrimental aspects of aid to needy children. They believed such assistance might erode the individual's independence and self-sufficiency. This fear is reflected in a 1928 Chicago Bureau of Child Study *Report* which commented on the black students' lack of adequate school clothing. The study noted that often school aid organizations could not meet the clothing demands of these children. The report observed, however, that even if this "paternalistic attitude" could be adopted, objections could be raised because such a policy "would tend to discourage a capacity for financial and social independence."[43]

Nevertheless, a movement arose to provide such services as school visitors, visiting nurses, penny lunches, and programs which would make the schools social centers within the community.

As early as 1904, Indianapolis employed a trained charity worker who served both as an attendance officer for the Negro schools and as "a friendly visitor for the home." The aims of the visitor were "to stimulate the interest of the parents in their children's school, to remove the prejudice of parents against colored schools and colored teachers, and to unite more closely the school and the home." The school system acknowledged that the main goal of the program was a modest one—namely, increased school attendance.[44] The results were proudly described in the 1908-1909 school report. Attendance in Negro schools increased from 89.2 percent in 1904 to 93.2 percent in 1909. The social gain, according to the report, was even greater. The director of truancy wrote that "the former hostility to colored schools and colored teachers has been almost entirely replaced by an increasing race pride in the schools, and by a growing consciousness that the school is working with the home for the best interests of the child."[45] Another result was an increase in enrollment in the parents' clubs connected with each school. This program illustrates the two distinct functions of educational officials such as school visitors. First, they attempted to mitigate some of the problems afflicting lower class students. For example, visiting teachers tried to help families set up home study areas for students, and visiting nurses and teachers often obtained medical aid for physically ill students.[46] One might argue that these school workers served a second purpose: to aid the victims of urbanization and racial prejudice in accommodating to their existing inferior position in the social hierarchy. In Indianapolis, for example, part of the purpose of the school visitor was to alter black parents' resentment of

segregated schools. Thus, these social workers served not only as agents
of altruism but also as agents of the status quo.

The development of parental interest and involvement in the schools
was also promoted through some school programs designed to make the
school a social center. The orientation of a black school in Indianapolis
indicated the emphasis on neighborhood involvement of many lower
class schools. At the request of the principal, the school board turned
over three tenement houses adjacent to the school which were to be torn
down. Students and neighborhood volunteers renovated the buildings
and converted them into social centers as well as classrooms. One became a demonstration home which housed the cooking and sewing
classes and was also open to neighborhood clubs as a social center. The
house served as an attractive model for the furnishing and decorating of
similar frame tenements in the area. One building was converted into a
gymnasium and boys' clubhouse which was open to the public in the
evenings. The school also maintained close contact with parents through
social and educational events to which the families were invited.[47]

Chicago schools followed a somewhat similar policy but also extended
the concept. The administration established community centers in schools
in low-income areas which opened the schools two nights each week for
organized recreational and social activities. Parents and children were encouraged to join in groups involving dramatics, physical education, athletics,
cooking, sewing, arithmetic, and English and music.[48] Formal accredited
classes through adult night schools were also provided in Chicago, Philadelphia, and Indianapolis.

The lack of parental involvement was a criticism frequently raised by
some teachers and principals. The Chicago Race Commission determined
that generally "the principals who found Negro parents unco-operative,
unambitious, and antagonistic were those who believed in separate schools,
found Negro children difficult to discipline, and would have no Negro
teachers in the schools."[49] Negro parents exhibited substantially less
involvement and cooperation with the schools than white middle-class
parents, but some teachers acknowledged that this lack of involvement
was the result of the large proportion of working Negro mothers.[50]
Negro parents also had difficulty in coming to school for conferences
with teachers or principals because it frequently meant the loss of pay.
Furthermore, Chicago principals found that Negro parents were more
interested and more ambitious for their children than were foreign parents.[51]

While all of the cities instituted programs of school visitors, visiting nurses, and other ameliorative efforts, there were never enough funds or inclination to alter significantly the conditions which handicapped Negro students. Schools also failed to adequately serve immigrants burdened by similar environmental conditions.[52] However, the educational response to the two groups during the period differed markedly. The schools exhibited greater flexibility in providing special programs to meet the immigrants' lack of preparation for the urban school, and they linked awareness of the immigrant with the educational and social goal of assimilation. Educators in these three cities, however, did not talk about assimilating the Negro into the mainstream of American life. In part, this differing emphasis may be explained in terms of the larger number of immigrants, the language barrier, and the fear that unassimilated immigrants threatened American society.[53] Another factor was that educators were far less convinced that blacks could or should be assimilated.

Either awareness or lack of awareness by educators of the effect of environmental factors on the educational performance of Negro students often had unfortunate results. On the one hand, the schoolmen's ignorance of home and community conditions which negatively affected the Negro child's progress reinforced in some educators' minds the belief in the inferiority of the race. This lack of understanding prompted statements like that of a Chicago teacher in 1920, who believed that Negro children "shut down" on their intellectual processes when they were about twelve or fourteen years of age.[54] In contrast, the more progressive educators acknowledged that environmental factors must be considered in understanding the black students' educational experience. Frances Blascoer argued this position throughout her report, concluding that "it seems clear that the needs of the colored school child who is backward or delinquent come chiefly from a wrong home environment, or from lack of care."[55] This recognition of the impact of environmental circumstances, however, allowed educators to excuse the schools and themselves from responsibility for the failure of the educational system in relation to their Negro students. In discussing the insidious qualities of the cultural deprivation position, Michael Katz has pointed out that it was as effective in removing responsibility from the schools for their failure as was the hereditary inferiority notion.[56] Thus, the schools were released from accountability for an indefinite period in the minds of many well-meaning reformers and educators. For instance, in 1902 Frances A. Kellor asserted: "The Negro child must be trained from infancy, his surroundings improved and the standards of his home life raised. Only then can the question be dealt with, 'What effect has education on the Negro?' "[57]

By 1920, many educators placed the burden of responsibility for the Negroes' poor scholastic performance on their unfortunate environment. They chose to ignore the fact that this explanation did not account for a pattern of accelerated retardation which appeared in almost all testing results of Negro children. If cultural deprivation were a significant contributing factor in retardation, presumably a child from such an environment would score further below the norms on tests of general intelligence and mental processes at six years of age, before he had exposure to the schools, than he would later in his educational career. Yet, the contrary situation consistently occurred. Howard Odum's study of Negro students in the Philadelphia schools illustrated this pattern of accelerated retardation. He found that Negro children of five, six, or seven years of age tested about normal but that the older children were far below normal. Black children entering school at five were 0.1 years above normal, while by the time the children were fifteen years old their mental age was only 11.3 years.[58] Part of this finding could be explained by suggesting that the unfortunate social conditions made an increasing impact on the child. But one could also question if the deterioration in performance was often not also in part attributable to the quality of the schools. Educators refused to accept this onus. Thus, if Negro children failed to meet the norms in reading achievement, the cause, according to the schoolmen, lay not in diluted curricula but in the fact that Negro students had few or no books at home.[59]

There is no question that the slums with all their related problems were demoralizing and destructive for Negro students. These environmental conditions do not, however, cover all of the negative forces which marked the educational experience of black children. The attitudes and assumptions which characterized the schools' relationship with their clients who were both black and from low socioeconomic backgrounds must be scrutinized further.

The power of environmental forces on Negro children suggests a further point which is perhaps more important than its connection to the halting scholastic progress of black children. These outside factors in the children's lives were so harsh, and their home and community environment so incongruous to the middle-class values espoused by the schools, that the school experience in many cases ultimately played little part in their lives. The minimal role of formal schooling in a child's broader education is probably a characteristic not only of Negro children's experience but also of other students from lower socioeconomic groups. For substantiation of the school's negligible role in a black child's life, one need only examine autobiographies of Negroes. Few books by black Americans describe formal education as having provided a vital learning experience. Rather the streets, the gangs, and the poverty-ridden crowded tenement flats or back alley shanties taught these children. Little that the schools provided brought promise to blacks that an education would alter these conditions. In fact, as the following two chapters suggest, educational policy in many cases helped perpetuate those conditions which locked black students into a future of menial jobs and minimal mobility.

NOTES

1. Frances Blascoer, *Colored School Children in New York* (New York: Public Education Association of the City of New York, 1915).

2. *Philadelphia Tribune*, March 23, 1912.

3. For an expansion of this position, see Colin Greer, *Great School Legend*, and Colin Greer, "Immigrants, Negroes and the Public Schools," *Urban Review* 2 (January 1969): 9-12.

4. Kelly Miller, "The Economic Handicap of the Negro in the North," *Annals of the American Academy of Political and Social Science* 27 (June 1906): 84.

5. Chicago Commission on Race Relations, *Negro in Chicago*, p. 362.

6. Chicago Public Schools, *Report of Child Study and Physical Examination of Teachers*, 1928-1929, p. 22.

7. Baker, *Following the Color Line*, pp. 131-132.

8. Henry J. Perkinson, *The Imperfect Panacea: American Faith in Education, 1865-1965* (New York: Random House, 1968), p. 57.

9. Emmett J. Scott, "Letters of Negro Migrants of 1916-1918," *Journal of Negro History* 4 (October 1919): 437.

10. Ibid., 432-433.

11. Louise DeKoven Bowen, *The Colored People of Chicago* (Chicago: Juvenile Protective Association, 1913), p. 3.

12. Richard R. Wright, Jr., *The Negro in Pennsylvania: A Study in Economic History* (Philadelphia: AME Book Concern, Printers, 1912), p. 190.

13. Andrew William Ramsey, "The Hoosier Negro Teacher," *Indiana Social Studies Quarterly* 18 (Spring 1964): 39.

14. N. C. Jenkins, "What Chance Has the Trained Student," in *The Negro in Chicago, 1779-1929* (Chicago: Washington Intercollegiate Club of Chicago, 1929), p. 89.

15. Ibid.

16. Baker, *Following the Color Line*, p. 112.

17. Mossell, "Standard of Living," pp. 194-195.

18. DuBois, *Philadelphia Negro*, p. 159.

19. Baker, *Following the Color Line*, p. 115.

20. While Table 4 does not include age-specific rates for the two races in the selected cities, comparisons of population distribution by age demonstrate that age distribution was notably similar in these cities for Negroes and whites. Therefore, the death rate statistics in the table are representative. See *U.S. Fifteenth Census, 1930*, Vol. 3, part 1, pp. 609 and 701, and part 2, p. 664.

21. Agnes P. Berry, "An Open Window Class," *Crisis* 9 (March 1915): 244.

22. Ibid., p. 245.

23. Thomas J. Woofter, *Negro Problems in the Cities* (Garden City, N.Y.: Doubleday, Doran and Co., 1928), p. 192.

24. Howard W. Odum, "Negro Children in the Public Schools of Philadelphia," p. 191.

25. Ibid.

26. Indianapolis Board of School Commissioners, *Annual Report*, 1908-1909, p. 9.

27. Edith Abbott and Sophonisba Breckinridge, *Truancy and Non-attendance in the Chicago Schools* (Chicago: University of Chicago Press, 1917), p. 147.

28. Ibid., p. 145.

29. Woofter, *Negro Problems in the Cities*, p. 194.

30. Ibid., p. 191.

31. Odum, "Negro Children in the Public Schools of Philadelphia," p. 188.

32. Iva Evelyn Smith, "Selected Case Studies of Dependent Negro Children in Their Relationship to the Public School: A Study of the Records of a Child Placing Agency" (M.A. thesis, University of Chicago, 1932), p. 84.

33. Louis R. Harlan, *Separate and Unequal* (New York: Atheneum, 1968), p. 208.

34. W.E.B. DuBois, ed., *The Negro Common School* (Atlanta, Ga.: University Press, 1901), p. 99.

35. Ibid., p. 100.

36. Ibid., p. 104.

37. Chicago Commission on Race Relations, *Negro in Chicago*, p. 265.

38. Most cities also provided these special ungraded rooms for immigrants who could not speak English.

39. Ibid., p. 267.

40. Clark Foreman, *Environmental Factors in Negro Elementary Education* (New York: W. W. Norton and Co., 1932), p. 13.

41. Ibid.

42. Smith, "Selected Case Studies," p. 196.

43. Chicago Public Schools, *Report of Child Study*, 1928-1929, p. 25.

44. Indianapolis Board of School Commissioners, *Annual Report*, 1908-1909, p. 9.

45. Ibid., p. 10.

46. Chicago Public Schools, *Report of Child Study*, 1928-1929, p. 26.

47. John and Evelyn Dewey, *Schools of Tomorrow* (New York: E. P. Dutton and Co., 1915), pp. 150-166.

48. *Chicago Defender*, February 20, 1926.

49. Chicago Commission on Race Relations, *Negro in Chicago*, pp. 250-251.

50. Ibid., p. 251.

51. Ibid.

52. See Greer, *Great School Legend*, pp. 80-129.

53. For the connection between the crusade for Americanization and American fear of the immigrants' effect on the society, see John Higham, *Strangers in the Land: Patterns of American Nativism, 1860-1925* (Rutgers, N.J.: Rutgers University Press, 1955).

54. Chicago Commission on Race Relations, *Negro in Chicago*, p. 249.

55. Blascoer, *Colored School Children*, p. 149.

56. Michael B. Katz, *Class, Bureaucracy and Schools*, p. 112.

57. Francis A. Kellor, *Experimental Sociology*, quoted in Colin Greer, *Great School Legend*, pp. 137-138.

58. Odum, "Negro Children in the Public Schools of Philadelphia," p. 201. Abraham Epstein commented on a similar development trend in his study of Negro students in Pittsburgh: "Practically all school principals stated that in the first four years the Negro child keeps well up with its white schoolmates, but that after the fourth grade, the Negro child often falls behind." Abraham Epstein, *The Negro Migrant to Pittsburgh* (Pittsburgh: University of Pittsburgh Press, 1918), p. 72.

59. For two discussions of this practice, see Kenneth B. Clark, "Clash of Cultures in the Classroom," *Integrated Education* 1 (August 1963): 8; and Raymond L. Jerrems, "A Sociological-Educational Study of a Public School in a Negro Lower-Class Area of a Big City" (Ph.D. dissertation, University of Chicago, 1965), p. 3.

3 EDUCATIONAL REFORM AND THE BLACK CHILD: INTELLIGENCE TESTING AND ABILITY GROUPING

The multitude of native white, immigrant, and black children pouring into the early twentieth-century school entered an institution undergoing profound transformation. Directed by dedicated schoolmen convinced of the necessity of a radical reorientation of the schools in order to meet the needs of an advanced technological society and a markedly heterogeneous population, American education embraced the Progressive movement's goals of professionalism, efficiency, and faith in science. The consequences included such educational reforms as the introduction of intelligence testing, classification of students in ability groupings, differentiated curricula, and vocational guidance. While the impact of these reforms often discriminated significantly against lower class and especially black children, one should be reminded of David Tyack's warning that "it makes little sense to malign the intentions of schoolmen in [these] campaigns" because "with few exceptions, their motives were good, their belief in the objectivity of their 'scientific' procedures manifest, their achievements in the face of massive challenges impressive."[1]

Educational reformers of the late nineteenth and early twentieth centuries revered scientific principles and were committed to establishing pedagogy as a true science. This quest for a scientific basis for education was evident in the plaintive observation of a Philadelphia district superintendent of schools in 1907 when he wrote: "Pedagogy will remain—well, pedagogy will remain pedagogy unless ways and means are devised and applied of testing our methods, processes, and results with an ever-increasing degree of accuracy."[2] New tools such as quantification and statistical measurement became valuable in applying the methods of scientific research to educational issues. One prominent educator who did graduate work in education and psychology at the University of Illinois during the period reminisced: "We lived in one long orgy of tabulation with the air . . . full of normal curves, standard deviations, coefficients, regression equations."[3]

It was inevitable that the Negro would be one of the groups which would undergo extensive measurement, testing, and scutiny by scientists and educators. Throughout the late nineteenth and early twentieth centuries, pioneers of science and pedagogy viewed Negro mental capacity as a vital issue in evaluating the race. Scientific studies initially centered around comparative analysis of Negro and Caucasian brains. However objective and scientific these scholars aspired to be, fundamental prejudices often colored their findings. One example of such an effect occurred in a highly publicized article in a respected journal in 1906. The paper was entitled "Some Racial Peculiarities of the Negro Brain." R. B. Bean, a Johns Hopkins scientist, compared the brains from Negro cadavers and white cadavers and determined that those of Negroes were significantly inferior in both weight and structure.[4] It was not until 1909 that one of Bean's colleagues at Johns Hopkins, F. B. Mall, made the same study with one exception. He identified the race of each of the samples only at the end of the experiment, rather than labeling them initially, as Bean had done. The differences Mall discovered between the brains were only negligible, and he concluded that personal values had influenced Dr. Bean's study. He asserted that no conclusions on the mentality of Negroes or whites could be made on the basis of brain structure or size.[5]

Other psychologists, skeptical of the validity of comparing cranial weight and structure, attempted to approach the question of Negro mental capacity through different means. M. J. Mayo based his doctoral dissertation at Columbia University in 1913 on a comparison of the scholastic grades of Negro and white children in New York City public schools. He acknowledged that school grades were not totally reliable but asserted that they were an acceptable measure because "there is a close correspondence between scholastic efficiency and intellectual capacity."[6] He was careful to point out that "mental differences between races, as between individuals are quantitative, not qualitative" and "that different rates of human progress and different degrees of civilization may be explained without the assumption of the mental inequality of different races and people."[7] Nevertheless, he concluded that Negroes were mentally inferior to whites because "the efficiency of colored pupils in the high school of the City of New York is about 3/4 of that of the whites."[8] Although many of the Negroes in the sample had recently arrived from the South, Mayo contended that this factor did not lower the Negroes' scholastic average. He assumed that only the most ambitious and the brightest migrated; therefore, if anything, the Negroes considered in the study could be considered above the average of their race.

Men directly involved in the application of the social sciences to education were making similar assessments about Negro mentality. One of the leaders in providing a scientific basis for educational principles was G. Stanley Hall, a psychologist who became a pioneer in child development as well as a noted president of Clark University. Not only did his numerous books influence a generation of educators, but also a journal he established, *Pedagogical Seminary,* was read by a large number of parents and teachers anxious to know of the latest educational theory.[9] Hall stressed that the child should not be fitted to the school as had traditionally been the case; rather, the school and the curriculum should be determined by principles of child development.[10] In designing a curriculum, great emphasis was laid on the various backgrounds and needs of the children.

Hall's work ultimately brought him to a consideration of the Negro's development. His analysis of the Negro would have great ramifications for any administrator or teacher following his tenet of molding the curriculum to the child. This pioneer in education believed that "no two races in history, taken as a whole differ so much in their traits, both physical and psychic, as the Caucasian and the African." The differences, he suggested, were so great that "what is true and good for one is often false and bad for another." He maintained that "many of these differences were naturally better understood in the days of slavery and the South than ever in the North or anywhere else."[11] In an article in *Pedagogical Seminary,* he dealt with the difference in the development of white and Negro children. His belief in "recapitulation," the concept that the child repeated the course of development of the race, influenced his view of blacks. According to Hall, Negroes, along with other "primitive races," had evolved only to the childhood or adolescence stage of racial development.[12] Therefore, Negro pupils could not be expected to advance as far as white students who were repeating the stages of a more developed race. He saw sexual development as an important influence on the ultimate mental inferiority of the Negro student. Up to the age of twelve, Negro children, according to Hall, were "quite as bright as the white child, but when this [sexual] instinct develops it is earlier, more sudden, and far more likely permanently to retard mental and moral growth than in the white who shoots ahead."[13]

Howard Odum, who had been a doctoral student of Hall at Clark University, was commissioned to do a special study of Negro children in the Philadelphia schools. He posited a similar theory when he discussed the poor scholastic performance of blacks as compared with whites in work past the eighth grade. He observed that "apparently the Negro children found it very difficult to go beyond their inheritance of simple mental processes and physical growth."[14] In discussing the causes for the Negro children's failure to apply themselves to their work, he cited "innate traits" and home and race influence.[15]

Other outstanding educational leaders of the period were similarly convinced of the inferiority of Negroes. Ellwood P. Cubberley, the force behind the rapidly growing Pedagogy and School Administration program at Stanford, author of some of the most popular textbooks on education, and one of the most influential educators as far as school administrators were concerned, had a low opinion of Negroes. In his model system of education for the fictitious state of Osceola, he included a provision for separate schools, if administrators desired, for the following groups: "the overaged, defective, delinquent, or the Negro race."[16]

Despite the general agreement on the mental inferiority of the Negro, the search continued for more accurate, more scientific means of measuring mental functions. In 1913, Mayo wrote: "Real progress can be made in this field of measuring mental ability only by a direct application of psychological tests or some other method of actually measuring mental phenomena."[17] The quest led many educators and scientists to acclaim the quantification of human intelligence and aptitude as the most scientific means of judging mental capacity. Intelligence tests were not a new invention—they had been used for limited experiments in the last years of the nineteenth century. Educators seized on them for extensive use, however, only after Alfred Binet and Theodore Simon developed the intelligence scale in 1906 as a means of identifying mentally retarded children for the French Department of Public Instruction. By 1908, Henry Herbert Goddard, a student of G. Stanley Hall, had translated Binet's intelligence scale and was using it to identify feeblemindedness.[18]

Testing for aptitude became a new area for American educators in the second decade of the twentieth century as Americans such as Edward Thorndike and Lewis Terman advanced in their research. Thorndike worked out measurements of aptitude in fields such as arithmetic, spelling, and language, while Terman refined Binet's test and introduced the idea of an intelligence quotient.

Before tracing the process by which measurement technology became entrenched in American education by the 1920s, one should consider the reasons educators and administrators enthusiastically endorsed intelligence testing in this relatively short period. First, the measurement of intelligence by tests seemed far more scientific and objective than any previous methods. Second, it was efficient: large numbers of students presumably could be tested quickly and orderly. Finally, testing was a valuable tool in rationalizing the existing social order. Like other native Americans, many progressive educators of the early twentieth century were besieged by fears that hordes of inferior southern and eastern Europeans and native blacks would overwhelm the superior Anglo-Saxons and undermine the nation's prevailing social order. Consequently, a number of the leaders in the educational testing movement also urged programs of Americanization, passage of eugenics laws, and immigration restriction.[19]

According to American educational psychologists such as Terman and Thorndike, the existing social structure should be protected because in large part it was based on merit—in other words, status and occupation in the United States reflected achievement and ability.[20] Furthermore, the leadership in this social hierarchy was marked not only by "men of superior intelligence," stated Thorndike, "but consequently of somewhat superior justice and good will." They acted, the tester believed, "in the long run, not against the interest of the world, but for it."[21] Thus, the preservation of the social order was desirable, these educators contended, because the system was enlightened and just. The schools therefore had a vital responsibility in developing and refining the meritocracy by measuring, grouping, and assigning students scientifically and efficiently.

Intelligence tests were valuable in preserving the social order because of what they measured—namely, the abilities valued by the society. Lewis Terman designed his widely used test to measure the skills he believed each level of occupations required. The most intelligence, he claimed, was necessary in the professions and "the larger fields of business."[22] Thus, one educator stated: "Little wonder the intelligence quotient reflected social-class bias! It was *based* on the social class order."[23] In his discussion of the influence of societal values on the definition of general intelligence, Russell Marks noted: "It is no exaggeration that in terms of environmental factors alone, tests measure what doctors and their sons do well, and what unskilled laborers and their sons do poorly."[24] As Clarence Karier has observed, Binet, Terman, Thorndike, and other educational psychologists acknowledged that "social class differences would not only influence the performance of any individual on a test, but that these differences were the very basis of the tests themselves."[25] For if one were convinced, as most testers were, that the upper classes were genetically superior, then this class orientation in the measurement of intelligence might be defended.[26]

The impact of these beliefs on the educators' evaluation of Negroes and others at the bottom of the social structure cannot be overemphasized. Even before intelligence tests were introduced in the schools on a mass scale, educational psychologists and other educators anxious to be involved in the forefront of scientific scholarship began a flurry of testing. Statistics on Negro children, along with native white and immigrant students, poured out of graduate schools, educational journals, and urban school systems in the second decade of the century. Some of the conclusions established that Negro children reached or excelled the median of white children, and some of the studies contemplated the thrust of adverse environment in I.Q. results, but the ultimate verdict was the same. The median I.Q. for Negroes was not as high as that for white children. Negroes were mentally inferior.

Edward Thorndike's article in *School and Society* announcing his findings on the intelligence score of Negro high school students was representative of the view of most people in the testing field around 1920. He stated that "less than 4 per cent of the colored pass the median white score for the corresponding grade." He concluded, "Whatever may be the theoretical possibilities of the negro race or of the white-colored hybrid, the actual negroes and hybrids now existent in this city showed a failure to include variations at the high-school age much above the level of the average white high-school pupil."[27] Thorndike considered this finding crucial because he saw the upper limit of a group as important as its average or typical status. An important factor concerning the black students which he measured was their attendance at an all-Negro school. Yet, he saw no reason to contemplate whether the training provided for these pupils might be unequal in quality to that of the white students and thereby skew the results.

These conclusions of measurement studies permeated pedagogy courses, graduate students' papers, and, ultimately, the classroom itself. For example, a doctoral candidate at the University of Pennsylvania who also taught in the Philadelphia schools wrote a dissertation on a predominantly Negro school in Philadelphia which was entitled "The Adjustment of a School to Individual and Community Needs." He stated, "With all the diversity of the conclusions of such prominent students of the subject— as Boas, LeBon, Hall, Galton, Thorndike, Woodworth, there is substantial agreement on the proposition that the negro is inferior to the white in the higher mental processes."[28] Thus, one of the conclusions of this student, who became the first director of the Bureau of Measurement and Research of the Philadelphia schools, was: "Studies of the psychology of the negro point to a somewhat lower average mentality, less subject to the inhibitions of higher mental powers."[29] This conclusion led him to propose a differentiated curriculum for the Philadelphia school which would be based on "an intimate knowledge of the pupils' capacity, ability and probable future development."[30]

The test results which gained the greatest attention became public following World War I. By 1917, the testing movement had advanced to the extent that the American Psychological Association offered to develop tests for the U.S. army to help classify the burgeoning army's recruits. The highly publicized results of this testing included the announcement that whites scored significantly higher than Negroes. Far less publicity was given to the fact that northern Negroes and whites scored higher than whites and blacks in the South.[31] The mass application of the army's Alpha and Beta tests opened an era of group testing which almost immediately inundated the schools. In the 1920s and 1930s, the measuring of students' abilities became a standard program in almost all major educational systems. The use of intelligence tests also provided a means of scientifically classifying and grouping by ability the heterogeneous mass of students in the schools. By 1926, the U.S. Bureau of Education reported that thirty-six of forty urban areas of 100,000 people or more used ability groupings in some or all grades, most based on intelligence scores.[32]

Intelligence testing received increasing attention among Chicago educators following World War I. As early as 1919, teachers read in the

Chicago Schools Journal, a house organ of the system, of the value of the Binet scale. The magazine extolled the virtues of "swiftness" and "accuracy" of the Stanford revision of the Binet scale and reprinted a section of Terman's *The Measurement of Intelligence* which explained the test's advantages. Terman claimed that an experienced tester "can in forty minutes arrive at a more accurate judgment as to a subject's intelligence than would be possible without the test after months or even years of close observation."[33] By 1921, the Chicago publication proclaimed that "teachers need to know how to talk in the language of our new scientific education," and surveyed various aspects of intelligence and its measurement.[34] In the following year, an article appeared in the publication entitled, "Can We Depend upon the Results of Group Intelligence Tests?" The author, a teacher in the Chicago Normal School, concluded that the results could be depended upon because, among other factors, a significant correlation existed between one's intelligence score and his position in life.[35]

Administrators began to introduce testing in the Chicago educational system in the early 1920s, and by 1926, all junior and senior high school students received group tests.[36] In the lower grades, the policy of testing varied from school to school. In the late 1920s, principals, teachers, or parent groups often had to finance the purchase of tests for an individual school.[37] Testing at the elementary school level was still not coordinated by 1932 because the *Report of the Survey of the Schools of Chicago, Illinois* condemned the "haphazard and sporadic programs of testing in some of the Chicago schools."[38] The Bureau of Child Study also provided testing services for individual pupils as well as some group measurement. The bureau relied on both the Terman revision of the Binet-Simon scale and tests devised by the bureau itself. The 1932 survey criticized the "homemade tests" because they had never been "subjected to statistical study for purposes of determining reliability or validity."[39] The survey report also warned that the bureau made many decisions on children on the basis of their performance on intelligence and achievement tests "without thorough acquaintance with all significant factors such as health, social problems, interests, and special abilities or disabilities."[40]

Chicago principals in lower class schools in which retardation rates were high used intelligence tests to support their nonpromotion policies and to defend their schools' efficiency. In 1928, the principal of an elementary school with a large black enrollment administered the Otis Intelligence Test to fifth and sixth graders and determined that their average

I.Q. was 86. He justified the school's high rate of nonpromotion by stating that many of the pupils had entered school late, were poorly prepared, and were correctly graded "from the standpoint of mental age."[41]

In Philadelphia, as well as in Chicago, administrators introduced intelligence testing in the 1920s. Increased use of such tests resulted in part from the prodding of a survey report of the school system in 1922. One of the chief criticisms the survey group leveled against Philadelphia's educational practices was the absence of classification of students according to ability. The report suggested that intelligence tests would aid educators in classifying pupils in homogeneous groups.[42] In the following years, Philadelphia incorporated such testing in the schools and expanded their testing staff to coordinate the program.[43]

Little information is available on testing in the Indianapolis schools during the post-World War I decade. By 1926, however, the city reported that intelligence tests were administered in all grades.[44]

Extensive use of intelligence measurement in American schools caused a few psychologists, educators, and laymen to begin to question the reliability of the tests and to wonder if too much faith was placed in their "scientific" results. Could it be the case, some observers of the testing movement queried, that performance on these tests might be affected by cultural deprivation or other environmental factors? As early as 1908, Binet acknowledged the importance of environmental opportunities as well as native intelligence, but Lewis Terman disagreed. In his widely read book *The Measurement of Intelligence,* Terman asserted that there was "no reason to believe that ordinary differences in social environment (apart from heredity), differences such as those obtaining among unselected children attending approximately the same type of school in a civilized community, upset to any great extent the validity of the scale."[45]

Some educators and psychologists questioned Terman. For a number of years, teachers and administrators had reported higher levels of retardation among students from impoverished backgrounds. It was not until 1935, when Otto Klineberg measured the intelligence quotients of Negro migrants, that the impact of environment on the intelligence scores of Negroes was fully recognized. In his landmark study *Negro Intelligence and Selective Migration,* Klineberg stated that there was "very definite evidence that an improved environment, whether it be the southern city as contrasted with the South as a whole or a northern city," raised the test score considerably. The rise in intelligence, this psychologist claimed,

was roughly proportionate to the length of residence in the more favorable environment. He countered the explanation of Mayo and others,
that only the superior blacks had the initiative to move north, by declaring that he saw "no evidence whatever in favor of selective migration."
In fact, he found that recent arrivals in the North scored no higher than
their southern counterparts.[46]

The issue of heredity versus environment continued to rouse educators
and psychologists to heated debate, but as Milton Schwebel contends, by
1925 the position of the schools on the issue was fairly well established.
According to Schwebel, most American educators chose to believe "that
mental ability [was] largely predetermined by the genes and largely im-
mutable by the time the child [came] to school. The school's task," he
asserts, was therefore "to classify, group, and offer instruction to help
the children reach their fixed potential."[47]

Adherence to the genetic theory and acceptance of the consistent reliability of intelligence measurement often made Negroes, some immigrant
groups, and other children of low socioeconomic status what David Tyack
has termed "victims without crimes."[48] Consequently, many Negro children migrating from the South were judged to be mentally handicapped.
In Philadelphia, these children were frequently sent to special schools and
were grouped as "deficient and socially incompetent."[49]

The consequences of the acceptance of the fixed I.Q. and the faith in
the validity of intelligence tests have been most significant in twentieth-
century education in America. Ellwood Cubberley noted the effects of
such beliefs in his introduction to Terman's *The Measurement of Intelligence*:

> The educational significance of the results to be obtained
> from careful measurements of intelligence of children can
> hardly be overestimated. Questions relating to the choice of
> studies, vocational guidance, schoolroom proceedings, the grad-
> ing of pupils, . . . all alike acquire new meaning and significance
> when viewed in the light of the measurement of intelligence.[50]

A less obvious consequence of intelligence testing than curriculum con-
siderations was the resulting attitude of teachers toward their students.
What were their expectations for children who tested below average? As
Schwebel comments, "A teacher who regards the current functioning of

the child as an adequate representation of his ability will expect and be content with the same level of performance."[51] The results of I.Q. tests often reinforced the teachers' preconceived opinions of Negro students. One teacher in the Chicago public schools voiced her agreement with the director of one of the special schools in the city which admitted children in part on the basis of low intelligence scores. The director had stated, "When a Negro boy grows a mustache his brain stops working."[52] A teacher with such an attitude would not likely encourage a Negro student in the upper grades; rather, she would expect very little. Black and white students in one Chicago school class learned from their instructor that the Alpha army tests proved that Negroes were intellectually inferior, and she cited figures and tabulations of other psychological tests to substantiate the assessment.[53]

The way teachers viewed their students and their learning capacity not only affected the teachers' evaluation of the students' mental capabilities but also influenced the students' views of their own abilities. Recent studies have indicated that if a teacher had low expectations for a child's intellectual capacity, the child's aspiration and performance level came to reflect that expectation. Investigators interviewing Chicago Negroes in the 1930s who were former students in the city's public school system discovered that teachers' unfavorable attitudes toward a pupil and their belief in the Negro's inferiority frequently became the child's view of himself. One girl with an I.Q. measured at 105 recalled such an experience and asserted, "It was the beginning of my inferiority complex at school and in the world." Another black pinpointed such an incident and claimed, "I became so unhappy I lost all my ambition in school and developed an absence of wholeheartedness."[54]

By the mid-1920s, some Negroes were aware of how intelligence tests could reinforce prejudices and also provide unreliable estimates of a student's ability or potential. As early as 1924, Horace Mann Bond, the noted black educator, held that in too many cases intelligence tests "have ceased to be scientific attempts to gain accurate information and have degenerated into funds for propaganda and encouragements for prejudice."[55] Black educators attacked the tests' inaccuracy in measuring native mental ability and also in determining the even more esoteric factor of native qualities which might make a student successful in the schools. Thomas Woofter's study refuted the reliability of intelligence quotients as a prediction of the academic achievement of Negro students by citing part of the *Twenty-fifth Annual Report of the Superintendent of Schools of New York City.* The superintendent described the administration's attempt to correlate intelligence quotients of teaching candidates with their scores on the written examination. The agreement between these two factors was judged in one case as "low" and in the other as "insignificant."[56]

Woofter argued that schoolmen frequently made assertions concerning I.Q.s and their importance which could not be substantiated. For example, a high school principal made a study of the causes of failure of twenty-seven of his black students. He concluded that "the intelligence quotients are alone enough to explain the major part of their failure," although fourteen of the pupils passed had lower intelligence quotients than the average for the twenty-seven who failed.[57]

In 1924, *Opportunity* published an article on a study made by Columbia University social workers which suggested certain problems in testing and determining the I.Q. of underprivileged Negro children. The social workers admitted that after testing Negro children it was "extremely difficult to gain a fair estimate of the mental ability of the children," partially because of the "unfavorable reaction of the students to educational group tests."[58] They described the self-consciousness of these students and their uncertainty about what was involved in testing. The testers revealed their hesitancy about placing great faith in the reliability of the intelligence tests to project a student's academic capability by pointing to the progress of several students who had "poor reactions to educational tests." One child had a mental test score of 45, which would be below the feebleminded level. Yet, he had entered school two years before and had kept up with normal students in his grade. The school reported that he had a general average for the entire period of "B" in work and conduct.[59]

Maudelle B. Bousfield, a noted teacher and the first Negro principal in Chicago, was also skeptical of the use of traditional I.Q. tests for deprived children and urged that "great caution should be exercised in attempting to index the mentality of any group, and certainly of an underprivileged group."[60] She justified this warning by noting that the results of three different mental tests showed significant variation. Furthermore, she wondered about the distortion of predicted I.Q.s on the basis of linguistic mental tests because when a nonlinguistic test was administered, students who had tested well below average on previous tests showed average or even above-average ability.[61]

There was little complaint by either white or black educators that the tests might be an inaccurate determinant of innate capacity because of white middle-class, culturally bound characteristics. Seldom did educators point out what one *Crisis* article declared: "A Negro child can hardly be expected to mark as 'true' the statement 'Silence must prevail in churches and libraries' when it is not true of churches he has attended."[62] Yet, the tests were filled with assumptions which had little correlation with the experience of a black child in a prejudiced society. For example, Terman's National Intelligence Test, published in 1920, included the following question which students answered by filling in the appropriate blanks:

Poverty cannot (*pull*) down a man (*who*) is intelligent and (*works*) hard.[63]

The Stanford Achievement Test included the following item to be completed:

If success is due in any one thing other than natural ability that thing is diligence, although it would be questionable to assert that either of these factors outweighs the other. Without native ability the most untiring worker may accomplish little of great value, and without (*diligence*) the mere possession of ability may not guarantee success in life.[64]

Most Negroes in the three cities remained silent about the use of intelligence tests during the 1920s, except when educators based segregation policies on test results. In Philadelphia, the local NAACP branch protested because administrators justified the grouping of Negro girls in a separate class at the prestigious Girls' High School on the basis of I.Q. scores.[65] The use of intelligence tests did, in fact, spawn another program which ultimately produced substantial segregation of lower class children, including blacks from others in the schools. This innovation was ability grouping of students by intelligence quotients. By 1926, 215 city school systems using group intelligence tests stated that the chief purpose was to classify pupils into homogeneous groups.[66] By the mid-1920s, all three cities had introduced ability grouping in some or all grades of the schools.

Philadelphia came under fire for its failure to classify elementary school students when the survey team studying the city's schools made its report in 1922. The experts argued for the division of elementary school pupils into three groups according to "physical fitness, intelligence, and previous attainment."[67] The study, recognizing that educators as well as parents might object to such a classification, attempted to respond to the major criticisms. To the objection "The plan is not democratic," the survey report responded, "This objection implies a misconception of democracy" because "true democracy in education means giving to each pupil, regardless of sex, race, creed, or economic status, the best educational opportunity that is possible." The report claimed that homogeneous groupings allowed students more opportunity than heterogeneous classes and were therefore more democratic. The survey team also dealt with the belief that "homogeneous classes remove the stimulating effect of the superior pupils from the average and inferior sections." That contention was countered with the assertion, "This loss is more than compensated for by the fact that in homegeneous sections, success depends on effort."[68]

Philadelphia administrators did not immediately respond to the recommendations by establishing a coordinated grouping system for all elementary school pupils. However, they did refine the ability groupings which already existed at the high school level. The intelligence quotients of students as well as their school marks became the basis for all classification in the high schools.

In Indianapolis, by 1926 schools grouped students according to ability in all twelve grades. They established three or more divisions for each grade, separating children according to their mental age as established by test scores and by teachers' judgments.[69]

Chicago practices of classification varied from school to school at the elementary level. Many elementary schools relied on extensive use of nonpromotion or acceleration of pupils in order to group students by ability. At the junior and senior high level, however, a more consistent policy of classification occurred. Administrators determined a pupil's mental age on the basis of his performance on an intelligence test and placed him in one of three or more groups.[70]

Although Negroes occasionally attacked the administering of intelligence tests, the use of ability groupings based on intelligence test results did not arouse great controversy within the black community. Even though it was the chief device for channeling students into various differentiated curricula, it generally went unnoticed by blacks or whites in the 1920s. Negroes who did contemplate the issue in the early years of the ability groupings' introduction into the schools often accepted the justification for the plan. As early as 1911, Cincinnati introduced special classes for particularly bright students. The *Chicago Defender* approved the plan and termed it "reasonable and based on common sense."[71] In 1923, a well-known Negro educator described the use of intelligence tests to track students and commented on its benefits. She did not criticize the grouping system, but instead observed, "These tests clarified the understanding of teachers as to the wide range of intelligence among Negro children."[72]

By 1930, intelligence tests and ability groupings were firmly established in the American educational system. They were viewed as reforms—as steps forward in the quest for a scientific basis for educational policy. Certainly they could offer educators some useful indexes of the academic strengths and weaknesses of particular students, but their awesome influence on educational policy and teachers' perceptions of students abilities must be lamented. To label an individual child as mentally deficient, slow, or a candidate for a nonacademic curriculum was not the problem, for some children did fall into these categories and needed special programs. The problem, rather, was to consistently brand the majority of a race with these terms, based on the culturally bound, imperfect early testing system. This educational reform frequently worked against Negroes as well as other lower class children in a subtle, quasiscientific manner. Its consequences were far more difficult to combat and far more pervasive than overt means of discrimination which black children might encounter in northern schools. All of the discrimination had one effect, however: to keep blacks in the schools as well as within the larger society in an inferior position. The ability grouping and the testing system reinforced another innovation, the differentiated curriculum, which is discussed in the following chapter. All three innovations contributed to the role of the schools as protector and perpetuator of the status quo.

NOTES

1. Tyack, *One Best System*, p. 181.

2. Oliver P. Cornman, "The Retardation of the Pupils of Five City School Systems," *Psychological Clinic* 1 (1907-1908): 257.

3. Harold Rugg, *That Men May Understand* (New York: Doubleday, Doran and Co., 1941), p. 82.

4. R. B. Bean, "Some Racial Peculiarities of the Negro Brain," *American Journal of Anatomy* 5 (September 1906): 353-433.

5. F. B. Mall, "On Several Anatomical Characteristics of the Human Brain Said to Vary According to Race and Sex," *American Journal of Anatomy* 9 (February 1909): 15-17, 20.

6. M. J. Mayo, "The Mental Capacity of the American Negro," *Archives of Psychology* 28 (1913): 10.

7. Ibid., pp. 51, 55.

8. Ibid., p. 42.

9. Lawrence Cremin, *The Transformation of the School: Progressivism in American Education, 1876-1957* (New York: Alfred A. Knopf, 1962), p. 102.

10. Ibid., p. 103.

11. G. Stanley Hall, "The Negro in Africa and America," *Pedagogical Seminary* 12 (September 1905): 358.

12. Dorothy Ross, *G. Stanley Hall, The Psychologist as Prophet* (Chicago: University of Chicago Press, 1972), p. 413.

13. Hall, "Negro in Africa and America," p. 358.

14. Odum, "Negro Children in the Public Schools of Philadelphia," p. 201.

15. Ibid.

16. Ellwood P. Cubberley, *State and County Educational Reorganization* (New York: Macmillan Co., 1914), p. 4.

17. Mayo, "Mental Capacity of the Negro," p. 62.

18. Clarence J. Karier, "Testing for Order and Control in the Corporate Liberal State," *Roots of Crisis*, p. 115.

19. See Clarence J. Karier, "Testing for Order and Control in the Corporate Liberal State"; also see Russell Marks, "Testers, Trackers and Trustees: The Ideology of the Intelligence Testing Movement in America, 1900-1954" (Ph.D. dissertation, University of Illinois, 1972), Ch. 2.

20. Marks, "Testers, Trackers and Trustees," p. 40; Clarence J. Karier, "Ideology and Evaluation: In Quest of Meritocracy," paper prepared for the Wisconsin Conference on Education and Evaluation, University of Wisconsin, Madison, April 26-27, 1973, p. 12.

21. Edward L. Thorndike, "Intelligence and Its Uses," *Harper's Monthly Magazine* 140 (January 1920): 235.

22. Lewis M. Terman, *Intelligence Tests and School Reorganization* (New York: World Book Co., 1923), pp. 27-28.

23. Karier, "Testing in the Corporate Liberal State," p. 121.

24. Marks, "Testers, Trackers, and Trustees," p. 3.

25. Karier, "Ideology and Evaluation," p. 12.

26. Ibid., p. 15.

27. Edward L. Thorndike, "Intelligence Scores of Colored Pupils in High Schools," *School and Society* 18 (November 10, 1923): 570.

28. Philip Albert Boyer, *The Adjustment of a School to Individual and Community Needs* (Philadelphia: By the Author, 1920), p. 35.

29. Ibid., p. 42.

30. Ibid., p. 103.

31. Milton Schwebel, *Who Can Be Educated?* (New York: Grove Press, 1968), p. 154.

32. "Cities Reporting the Use of Homogeneous Groupings, the Winnetka Technique and the Dalton Plan," *City School Leaflet*, No. 22 (Washington, D.C.: U.S. Bureau of Education, December 1926), p. 2.

33. "The Stanford Revision and Extension of the Binet Tests," *Chicago Schools Journal* 2 (December 1919): 9.

34. *Chicago Schools Journal* 3 (December 1921): 315.

35. Denton L. Geyer, "Can We Depend upon the Results of Group Intelligence Tests?" *Chicago Schools Journal* 4 (February 1922): 204.

36. "Cities Reporting the Use of Homogeneous Groupings," p. 3.

37. George D. Strayer, *Report of the Survey of the Schools of Chicago, Illinois*, Vol. 2 (New York: Bureau of Publications, Teachers College, Columbia University, 1932), p. 108.

38. Ibid.

39. Ibid., p. 114.

40. Ibid., p. 113.

41. Don C. Rogers, "Retardation from the Mental Standpoint," *Chicago Schools Journal* 9 (April 1927): 302-303.

42. Pennsylvania State Department of Public Instruction, *Report of the Survey of the Public Schools of Philadelphia*, Vol. 2 (Philadelphia: Public Education and Child Labor Association of Pennsylvania, 1922), p. 288.

43. W. S. Deffenbaugh, "Research Bureaus in City School Systems," *City School Leaflet*, No. 5 (Washington, D.C.: U.S. Bureau of Education, January 1923), pp. 18-19.

44. "Cities Reporting the Use of Homogeneous Groupings," p. 3.

45. Lewis M. Terman, *The Measurement of Intelligence* (Boston: Houghton Mifflin Co., 1916), p. 116.

46. Otto Klineberg, *Negro Intelligence and Selective Migration* (New York: Columbia University Press, 1935), p. 59.

47. Schwebel, *Who Can Be Educated?*, pp. 66-67.

48. Tyack, *One Best System*, p. 217.

49. *Philadelphia Tribune*, October 31, 1929.

50. Ellwood P. Cubberley, in Lewis Terman, *Measurement of Intelligence*, pp. vii-viii.

51. Schwebel, *Who Can Be Educated?*, p. 66.

52. Chicago Commission on Race Relations, *Negro in Chicago*, p. 439.

53. Horace Mann Bond, "Intelligence Tests and Propaganda," *Crisis* 83 (June 1924): 62.

54. Albert Sidney Beckham, "A Study of Race Attitudes in Negro Children of Adolescent Age," *Journal of Abnormal and Social Psychology* 29 (April-June 1934): 24.

55. Bond, "Intelligence Tests and Propaganda," p. 61. See also Bond, "Some Exceptional Negro Children," *Crisis* 24 (October 1927): 257-259, 278, 280.

56. *Twenty-fifth Annual Report of the Superintendent of Schools of New York City*, 1923, pp. 25-26, quoted in Woofter, *Negro Problems in Cities*, p. 189.

57. Woofter, *Negro Problems in Cities*, p. 189.

58. Walter R. Chivers and Mabel E. Bickford, "Overage Negro Children," *Opportunity* 2 (May 1924): 150.

59. Ibid.

60. Maudelle B. Bousfield, "The Intelligence of Negro Children," *Journal of Negro Education* I (October 1932): 375.

61. Ibid.

62. Edith M. Stern, "Jim Crow Goes to School in New York," *Crisis* 44 (July 1937): 202.

63. L. M. Terman and others, *National Intelligence Test* (Yonkers, N.Y.: World Book, 1920), Scale A, Form 1, Question 19, quoted in Marks, "Testers, Trackers, and Trustees," p. 36.

64. L. M. Terman, T. L. Kelley, and G. M. Ruch, *Stanford Achievement Test* (Yonkers, N.Y.: World Book, 1923), Advanced Exam, Form B, p. 5, quoted in Marks, "Testers, Trackers and Trustees," p. 37.

65. *Philadelphia Tribune,* February 16, 1924.

66. W. S. Deffenbaugh, "Uses of Intelligence and Achievement Tests in 215 Cities," *City School Leaflet,* No. 20 (Washington, D.C.: U.S. Bureau of Education, March 1925): 1.

67. *Report of the Survey of the Public Schools of Philadelphia,* II, 287.

68. Ibid., pp. 288-289.

69. "Cities Reporting the Use of Homogeneous Groupings," p. 3.

70. Ibid.

71. *Chicago Defender,* May 13, 1911.

72. Elise Johnson McDougald, "The School and Its Relation to the Vocational Life of the Negro," *Hospital Social Service* 8 (1923): 18.

4 EDUCATIONAL REFORM AND THE BLACK CHILD: THE CURRICULUM

Public School No. 26 stood in the midst of the poorest section of Indianapolis. Clustered around the dilapidated main building were three renovated tenement shacks housing the domestic science and manual training classes. Yet, this externally unimpressive all-black school achieved national prominence when John and Evelyn Dewey hailed it as one of the "schools of tomorrow" in their 1915 book.[1] What did this school offer which made it an exemplar of progressive education? What did its highly praised curriculum reveal about the attitudes of twentieth-century reformers toward the role of the school vis-à-vis various groups in the community, especially black Americans? And finally, what can scrutiny of curricular reforms indicate about educators' visions of the Negro's role in an advanced urban industrial society?

The program and services of P.S. 26 reflected several canons of progressive reform. First, according to the renowned educator and his daughter, the school recognized the special characteristics of its impoverished clientele and had introduced an "entire reorganization [of the curriculum] to meet the needs of the children of the community, physically, intellectually, and socially."[2] This concept of fitting the school to the particular needs of the students by differentiating the curriculum had begun by 1900 and had marked an important alteration in the goals and functions of the school.

In the nineteenth century, schools had offered a rigidly uniform lock-step curriculum for all students. The common school had embodied Horace Mann's concept that all children should have the same training in minimal skills so that students might be able to begin competing in the world outside the classroom on an equal footing. Reformers now condemned this common curriculum as rigid, inefficient, and "undemocratic" because they contended it met the needs of only a small portion of the clients crowding into the schools as a result of the new compulsory education laws.[3] The same curriculum that served middle-class children in the newly developing streetcar suburbs was not appropriate for children coming from the overflowing ethnic and racial ghettos. These reformers were convinced that the residents of these contrasting areas had starkly different experiences—and the schools must move to reflect "the distinct educational needs" of each part of society.[4]

Ellwood P. Cubberley of Stanford bluntly stated one argument for the new role of the schools in *Changing Conceptions of Education:*

> Our city schools will soon be forced to give up the exceed-
> ingly democratic ideal that all are equal, and that our society is
> devoid of classes, as a few cities have already in large part done,
> and to begin a specialization of educational effort along many
> new lines in an attempt better to adapt the school to the needs
> of these many classes in city life.[5]

While Dewey and his daughter would have been at odds with Cubberley's antidemocratic impulses, they did applaud the idea of a broadened curriculum to meet the individual's and the community's needs.

The Indianapolis school they admired reflected this belief that the children from the surrounding destitute area required different training from that appropriate to middle-class children. At the core of the school's efforts to meet the particular needs of the neighborhood and its children was the practical training which dominated the revised curriculum. Students in all grades spent many hours each week in domestic science classes learning cooking, sewing, millinery, and crocheting or in manual arts classes. In fact, these children spent twice as much time in domestic and industrial training courses as did students in white schools in the Hoosier capital.[6]

The heavy dose of industrial training which P.S. 26 students received was typical of the special differentiated curriculum in many lower class schools in which the workshop and the kitchen became important educational centers. This type of practical and industrial training gained supporters for numerous reasons. Some pedagogical reformers hailed it as the only type of instruction suited to the ability of the lower-class students. Educators of this ilk had a vivid image of these new clients. G. Stanley Hall referred to them as "the great army of incapables in the school."[7] Because of their presumed mental capabilities and their destiny in the industrial order, the classic academic program was not appropriate.

The proponents of industrial training were influenced not only by their conception of the needs of these children but also by the demands of an advanced industrial society. The increasing differentiation and specialization of work in industrial America required dutiful trained workers. Sol Cohen, quoting leading educators of the period, has observed: "What the new industrial order needed was 'the training of recruits for our leading mechanical industries'; the services of an army of semiskilled workers who would 'adjust nicely [to] the industrial machine.' "[8]

Other educators saw practical training as a means of curbing the astronomical dropout rate of students fleeing the upper grades because of boredom with the traditional curriculum. They argued that vocational programs would keep students in school longer, give them a marketable skill, and help them advance in a society demanding more training.

While educators and businessmen hailed vocational education as desirable for many white students, they considered it even more appropriate for black students. Such a curriculum with a strong emphasis on non-academic courses which would turn out docile workers and moral citizens fulfilled what many educators had been seeking for Negro children—a special type of education. As Doxey Wilkerson observed, "American minority education has commonly proceeded upon the assumption that people of inferior status require special types of education."[9] Writing in 1923, one black educator charged white educators with "still [being] dazzled to a large extent by a one sided programme of vocational education for all Negroes."[10]

The rise of vocational education as a desirable choice for Negroes was not championed and promoted merely by white educators. From the 1870s onward, many blacks heralded industrial training as a means of racial uplift.[11] Not only in the South where industrial education became virtually the only type of black education acceptable to whites, but also in the North, industrial training gained black supporters. Fanny Jackson Coppin, for instance, principal of Philadelphia's prestigious Institute for

Colored Youth, became an early proponent of industrial training and moved quickly in the 1880s to see that the institute offered both the traditional academic curriculum and a well-developed industrial arts program.[12] Many Negroes in the early twentieth century, influenced by the race's leading spokesman, Booker T. Washington, were also enthusiastic about industrial education programs. The *Indianapolis Freeman* was long an advocate of industrial training. In 1901, the newspaper praised "the Booker T. Washington theory of education" because it "meets the exigencies of the day."[13] Thus, progressive educators anxious to have education "fit the needs of the child" found supporters for practical training among both races.

Not all educators, white or black, were enamored with practical and industrial training in the public schools. Early in the crusade for such programs, the esteemed William Torrey Harris, St. Louis superintendent of schools in the 1870s and later U.S. commissioner of education, argued that such training did not adequately develop the higher faculties of the student. W.E.B. DuBois echoed similar sentiments after the turn of the century and contended that the industrial curriculum proposed for his race was often "caste education."[14] But such critics were in the minority, and by World War I, vocational education was not only offered in the upper grades but also reached far down into the elementary grades.

According to the reformers, children from non-WASP backgrounds needed a curriculum emphasizing vocational skills and socialization as well. Many schoolmen believed that the immigrants from southern and eastern Europe and native blacks were children of inferior intellectual and social backgrounds who must be socialized for America's sake as well as their own. Less attention was centered on the incoming blacks because, as Chapter 2 suggests, they were fewer in number and also did not have the language barrier. However, this "child race," a term often used by administrators, had, according to the educators, some of the same problems and deficiencies as the immigrant. Because educators based their programs for both groups on similar assumptions, the way the differentiate curriculum affected blacks was not unlike the effect on poor whites, although racism unquestionably complicated the Negro child's experience.

The curriculum which educators proposed for these lower class children incorporated so much socialization that Michael Katz has maintained that the main purpose of the lower class schools became "noncognitive." He defines this term as "the inculcation of the norms and attitudes thought essential to orderly, moral urban living." Katz also alleges that many of the goals of socialization had "a class flavor" because they represented "what the 'better' part of the community . . . thought necessary to civilize the rest."[15] At P.S. 26, for example, the Deweys noted approvingly that the school emphasized activities that developed thrift, tidiness, cleanliness, and ambition. They observed, "Inside the school pupils are taught higher standards of living than prevail in their homes."[16]

The socialization concerns are evident in the curricula of all three cities. For example, one Philadelphia elementary school which taught lower class children, half of whom were black, emphasized practical household economy, bodily cleanliness, orderliness, neatness, wise purchasing, "sane decoration," cooking, sewing, and child hygiene as desirable parts of the regular school work.[17] The 1916 *Annual Report* of the Indianapolis schools proclaimed that, as a consequence of the domestic arts courses, Negro girls showed "better taste in the selection of harmonious and becoming colors."[18] One might argue that such training was needed by children coming from impoverished backgrounds, but often such programs received more attention than basic skills such as reading, writing, and arithmetic, historically the prime concern of the school.

What is critical to recognize about much of the curricular variation introduced in the lower class school was the barrier placed on the possible mobility of the child. In the past, socialization by the schools had included at least implicit provisions for upward mobility and encouragement of students' aspirations. Now educators questioned such a goal for the schools. In 1906, one member of the faculty of Columbia University Teachers College said: "If the chief object of government be to promote civic order and social stability, how can we justify our practice in schooling the masses in precisely the same manner as those who are to be our leaders?"[19] Thus, the desire for civic order, social stability, and social efficiency, as well as perceptions of the blacks' presumed intelligence level and particular educational needs, figures prominently in the move to establish a special curriculum for Negroes.

In Philadelphia, the first notice of the administration's desire to alter the curriculum for all Negro students appeared in 1907 in the *Annual Report of the Superintendent.* Regarding Negro students, Martin G. Brumbaugh stated:

> I do not purpose [*sic*] at this time to discuss the materials
> of the curriculum as they relate to the different type of

children that attend our public schools, but I believe that
sooner or later there will such a differentiation of the
subject matter of the curriculum and such modification
of the course of study as to make more effective the
discipline and education these pupils should receive.[20]

Other educators, noting the increasing number of black pupils in Philadelphia, concurred. In 1913, Howard Odum's study of Negro children
in Philadelphia public schools echoed similar sentiments. He cited the
poor environmental condition of Negro students, their performance on
intelligence tests, and their retardation which, he alleged, produced the
"lack of adaptation of children to the curriculum [that] is costing the
community thousands of dollars annually and is at the same time a hin-
drance to school efficiency and progress." He therefore argued for a more
"proper education" and vocational education and guidance for the Negro
children.[21] In "Retardation in the Elementary Schools of Philadelphia,"
Byron A. Phillips wrote that "in the case of the negro, it seems that the
curriculum at present is entirely unfitted to his capabilities." Thus, his
proposed solution was to organize all-Negro schools in the city with a
special course of study.[22]

In fact, a pilot program of what Philadelphia educators deemed a proper
education for Negroes was already operating, for it had been introduced
in the James Forten School in 1896. By 1890, the Forten School, the first
public school established in Philadelphia for Negroes, had become known as
"one of the poorest in the city: it does not interest the children."[23]
Attendance had declined to such an extent that the board planned to
close Forten. A prominent Philadelphia matron who was a member of the
board of public education persuaded the board to assume direct management of the school and to revise the curriculum and make it a manual
training school at the elementary level. About half of the student body
was Negro; the rest came mainly from Russian Jewish immigrant families.
Instruction in sewing and cooking for girls and woodworking and sloyd
for boys was offered from the early grades.

Despite the alleged success of the school, the percentage of black
pupils continued to decline, as a result of shifting patterns of racial
groups in the neighborhood and, according to one Philadelphia educator,
"the character of the ignorant class of colored people who remain near
the school."[24] This loss of Negro student body was lamented because,
according to the same educator:

The manual work has a decidedly stimulating effect upon the
sluggish colored child. In comparison with the alert Russian
Jew, the negro child of the slums seems heavy and stupid,
but measured by the standards of the race the results justify
the claim that this school is peculiarly adapted to the education
of the colored child.[25]

Philadelphia Negroes were ambivalent about a strong emphasis on manual training and vocational education for their children. On one hand,
several leaders of the black community had been closely involved with the
expansion of practical training for Negroes in private schools. Besides Fanny
Jackson Coppin's efforts at the Institute for Colored Youth in the late
nineteenth century, Reverend Matthew Anderson, pastor of Berean Presbyterian Church, helped found the Berean School in 1899, a trade school,
and was a staunch friend of vocational training for blacks.[26] Another
local minister, Reverend William Creditt, established Downington Industrial School in 1904, a boarding school located near the city.[27] One of the
strongest pleas for increased industrial training came from a future bishop
of the African Methodist Episcopal church, Reverend Richard R. Wright,
Jr., in his dissertation at the University of Pennsylvania on the economic
and social conditions of blacks in that state. "At present," he wrote in
1912, "the most useful things that Negro children are taught, are to be
had in reformatory and special schools." In his description of the dire
need for industrial education for Negroes, he hastened to point out that,
although he was discussing the needs of the average child, this program
did not apply to all Negro children. Observing that social and economic
stratification was developing in black society, he stated, "The son of the
Negro physician who has both economic opportunity and a good home
life, does not need all that the son of the illiterate Negro laborer needs."[28]
Thus, both blacks as well as whites saw social class distinctions as important
determinants in the type of education a child received.

Other Negroes were wary of any intensified vocational education program and labeled such plans as a "serious obstacle to Negro children's
aspirations for higher education and as evidence of greater acceptance
in the North for Booker T. Washington's general philosophy."[29]

When, in 1915, the black community learned of Department of Vocational Education and Guidance plans which they believed would ultimately
"vocationalize the separate black grade schools," they reacted with con-

cern. A group of Negroes met with board members on two different occasions to ascertain what the ramifications of the plan would be. Their anxiety was twofold: first, they feared this move might be the precursor of more segregation in the schools, which was already a source of great concern to them; second, they wanted to determine what educational principles were involved in vocational training. At one meeting of leading Negroes, the group which met with the school administrators reported that the board officials assured them that the plan would not involve the establishment of a separate high school. They also informed the concerned blacks that the special training would be inaugurated in all the grades below high school as "a remedy for the condition of the colored children" and for the retardation which existed among Negro students. The secretary of the board stated that black parents who objected to the curriculum could send their children to white schools.[30]

The Negroes were skeptical and resentful. One minister reminded the blacks of an incident at one of the local high schools when a Negro spoke at a meeting restricted to the black students. He had directed the pupils to urge their parents to allow them to take the high school vocational education curriculum. Other blacks were similarly outraged, and a group was established to fight the board's move and to investigate the issues further.[31]

In a forceful *Crisis* editorial, W.E.B. DuBois supported the opposition of Philadelphia blacks to the proposed expansion of industrial training. He explained that the resistance occurred because the Negroes recognized "that if their children are compelled to cook and sew when they ought to be learning to read, write, and cipher, they would not be able to enter the high school or go to college as the white children are doing."[32]

The board announced that the vocational education plan would be introduced first at Thomas Durham School, the largest segregated school in the city. It would begin by providing vocational training for four hundred of the twelve hundred students enrolled at the school. Allegedly, if the plan were successful, similar programs would follow in the other separate schools. The ultimate outcome is unclear. Vocational education offerings increased in both black and white schools, but at no time was this curriculum mandatory for all black children. Negro students attending several of the separate black schools did, however, receive domestic arts training a year longer than any white students in the city.[33]

In 1922, the Philadelphia school survey further encouraged this pattern by urging that the curriculum for overage pupils be altered in order to provide more "handiwork of a prevocational type."[34] This recommendation would affect a large number of black students because the survey singled out Negroes as responsible for the high percentage of overageness in the Philadelphia schools. The study asserted that "adaptation of the curriculum and teaching methods to racial differences" was feasible because many of the black pupils were segregated.[35]

Philadelphia Negroes remained wary of some of the underlying goals of avid proponents of vocational education and a modified curriculum for blacks. In 1927, the *Tribune* carried a discussion of a Philadelphia educator's speech advocating vocational education as a means of improving workers' morals as well as their efficiency. The newspaper characterized her as "one of the best exponents of the status quo in education as represented by the conservative agencies in education in America today."[36]

The modified curriculum for black students remained only a partially realized goal of Philadelphia educators. In Indianapolis, however, administrators were able to implement on a citywide basis a significantly diluted academic curriculum for Negroes. In Indianapolis schools, the curriculum for the separate black schools provided twice as much industrial training as pupils received in the white schools—in all of the eight primary grades.[37] The city, which prided itself on having one of the most progressive school systems in the nation, had introduced vocational education programs in the schools by the turn of the century. Significantly, the Negro schools were the first ones to be provided with industrial departments.[38]

Vocational training offerings in the lower grades expanded substantially in the first decade of the twentieth century, particularly in grades seven and eight, so that students who were not likely to remain in school beyond the period of compulsory attendance might be better prepared. The assistant superintendent stated that this plan was especially geared to "those who are more or less retarded."[39] The program was designed to give them definite training that "will prepare them for the special work which they are to undertake." Printing was added for boys and advanced sewing for girls, as well as two activities for both sexes, weaving and pottery. It is not clear how weaving and pottery could prepare the students for employment needs in Indianapolis. According to the assistant superintendent, the introduction of this expanded vocational education program had required modification of the regular school studies, but "the minimum essentials, so far as they could be approximately determined, were retained."[40]

Indianapolis planned to extend vocational education even further in the primary grades by 1916. The assistant superintendent of the primary grades explained that vocational training was increasing because part of the criterion in determining a child's education was "what the community expects him to become."[41] In the same report, the administrator noted that this increased vocational training program in the primary grades was particularly desirable for those students "unable to respond readily to lessons in reading and kindred language subjects."[42] Thus, if a child had trouble with basic skills such as reading, the solution was not to give the child more intensive work in remedial reading but to lessen the work in reading and give him vocational training in the primary grades.

DuBois, the most articulate critic of vocational education as the main curriculum for Negroes, experienced a cool reception in Indianapolis by members of both races when he visited there in 1912. DuBois declared in a speech in the city that Negroes should strive to provide all their children with the "largest possible amount of general training and intelligence before teaching them the technique of a particular trade." He also stressed his familiar belief in the need of higher education for the future leaders of the race.[43] According to DuBois, the *Indianapolis Star,* a white newspaper, denounced his speech as "dangerous." The supervisor of the Negro schools of Indianapolis wrote the *Crisis* editor, expressing his regret that DuBois' lecture had attacked his school curriculum and ideals.[44]

In the *Crisis,* DuBois defended his position and provided a revealing critique of many of the values enunciated by the Indianapolis schools. He wrote: "When a proud principal of a school shows workshop and kitchen, table and pie, one may be interested, but one is no more convinced than when another shows an array of Greek roots and rounded phrases." He suggested the ultimate goal of education was "neither the table nor the phrase—it is the boy." He demanded to know if the boys trained there were intellectually challenged and had some knowledge of the world they lived in. "Are they trained in such ways as to discover their true bent and ability, and to be intelligently guided to the choice of a life's work?" Finally, DuBois attacked the pressure groups which actively supported expansion of the vocational education in the primary grades. These people believed, he lashed out, that "Indianapolis exists for the sake of its factories and not the factories for the sake of Indianapolis." He asserted that "what with impudent maids, and half trained working men, they are tired of democracy; they want caste; a place for everybody and everybody in his father's place with themselves on top, and 'Niggers' at the bottom where they belong."[45]

Few Indianapolis blacks were prepared to fully accept DuBois' message because, throughout the period, most of the city's Negroes favored the emphasis on vocational education in black schools.[46] At a meeting in 1909 between some of the members of the school board and a delegation of black ministers, the Negroes approved of the administration's plan to expand vocational training in the lower grades. Several ministers observed that it was "better for a girl to earn a diploma by learning to make her own graduation dress than by a brilliant essay on "The Royal Path of Life."[47] In 1919, the Negro newspaper, the *Indianapolis News,* declared that the public schools should provide more extensive offerings in industrial and vocational training for Negro children in the grammar grades.[48]

In 1917, George Hayes, supervising principal of the colored schools of Indianapolis, gave a speech before the National Society for the Promotion of Industrial Education which embodied the attitudes of many of the city's blacks toward vocational education. Hayes cited the establishment of more vocational classes as an important means for Negroes to overcome their previous limited occupational training and to compete more effectively with trained whites for jobs. He rejected the concept of special training for Negroes which was different from that of whites. Appealing to the educational survey groups studying school systems and encouraging expanded vocational training, he beseeched them not to "hamper or embarrass" the Negro "by recommending special courses to meet his particular needs," but instead to give him a chance to become a trained workman, "not a Negro workman."[49] The message was optimistic and what many observers of the period would term realistic. How many new vocational opportunities such training would provide was uncertain because, while Hayes gave some encouragement to Negroes to investigate new fields of employment, he placed greater emphasis on better training for the fields in which Negroes were already engaged as janitors, butlers, and cooks.

There were some exceptions to the blacks' general acceptance of the heavy emphasis on vocational training in the Negro schools. In 1914, a black mother hired an attorney to request that the board of education grant her daughter permission to transfer from a black school to one which was not "exclusively vocational." In denying the request, the superintendent rejected the characterization of the black school and claimed that with certain exceptions its curriculum was very similar to that of white schools.[50] Thus, neither black parents who objected to their children's curriculum nor a national figure such as W.E.B. DuBois could alter or dislodge the Indianapolis schools' discriminatory policy in the curriculum for Negro students.

By 1920, the trend in both Indianapolis and Philadelphia was clear. Vocational education would not remain in the seventh, eighth, and high school grades. It would be offered throughout the school years for children from lower class homes—and particularly for black students. DuBois struck out at such programs for the elementary schools in the *Crisis*. He asserted that in the first four years of a child's education—regardless of his race or condition—the curriculum should be limited to reading, writing, and mastering fundamental mathematical procedures. "No vocational training has any place in a primary school," he thundered. "Any attempt to turn the primary school into a place for teaching trades or teaching agriculture or teaching housework as such is absolutely wrong and should be fought bitterly by every advocate of democracy and human uplift."[51] He acknowledged that out of necessity some children aged ten to fourteen might have to take some vocational work for self-support, but he argued that "no nation as rich and as enlightened as the United States could afford to make this necessary."[52]

The existence of expanded practical training in the elementary grades in Chicago made that city as well as Indianapolis and Philadelphia vulnerable to DuBois' attack. However, Chicago's policy was unlike that of the other two cities in one respect. Because there was no official distinction between the black and white students, or the predominantly black or white schools, the board of education initiated no special curricula for Negroes. Within individual classrooms, however, the type of material did vary, depending on the teacher's attitudes. Thus, the committee investigating the causes of the 1919 race riot interviewed a teacher in an elementary school who proclaimed that "colored children are restive and incapable of abstract thought; they must be constantly fed with novel interests and given things to do with their hands." The committee observed that children under such teachers were accordingly given handicrafts instead of arithmetic and singing instead of grammar.[53]

This approach was not an isolated one, for in 1916 the *Defender* demanded of its readers: "Do you know what your child is learning at
school? Do you know whether her education or his education is the same
as that of some other child who attends another school in a different part
of the city?" The article then went on to cite cases of predominantly black
schools that appeared to offer a diluted academic curriculum in comparison
with other schools in the city. A child who attended Ferrin School, which
had a majority of black students, explained that the teacher read stories
to the children each day and required no homework. When the child transferred to another school and the teacher learned she had attended Ferrin,
she told the girl: "Oh, that isn't up to the standard. If you go to school
here you will have to study. There are books in the library if you want to
read stories, but you will have a certain amount of homework to do." The
Defender asked, "Does the board of education stand for a distinction of
classes?"[54]

Official curriculum changes became a heated issue in Chicago between
1913 and 1917 when the city debated the advisability of a proposed rigid
two-track system. It was not, however, a question which riveted the Negro
community's attention. The debate arose after the Commercial Club, an
organization of business and industrial leaders of the city, asked former
superintendent of schools Edwin G. Cooley to go to Europe, study vocational education there, and suggest to Chicago appropriate educational
policy in this area. Cooley proposed a plan patterned after the European
system of two separate curricula, one general and one vocational, which
would be offered in separate schools beginning at the seventh grade.[55]
Each curriculum would be administered by a separate board of education
and superintendent. A special tax would be required, and a bill providing
for the plan would have to pass the state legislature.

Many pressure groups and organizations within the city squared off in
support or opposition. Those favoring the plan included commercial and
industrial groups such as the Illinois Manufacturers' Association, the Commercial Club, the Industrial Club, and the City Club.[56] Opposing the bill
were the majority of teachers, organized labor, and various civic groups. The
opponents of the Cooley Bill charged that it was "a poorly masked attempt
to split the American system of education, reduce the general educational
opportunities of the masses, and fasten upon the state of Illinois the caste
system of the Old World."[57] Opponents also accused employers of sup-

porting the bill because it would provide them with an unlimited number of docile laborers, trained at state expense.

This plan would obviously have consequences for the majority of lower class children, including Negroes. The black community, however, was curiously silent. Chicago Negroes generally supported vocational training because they believed it provided students with skills which would make them more able to compete for jobs; they therefore dismissed the class implications of the program.[58] Throughout the period, the *Chicago Defender* praised vocational training because of its practicality. Robert Abbott, the respected publisher of the *Defender,* observed that "there is no question but what a boy or girl who learns to do things with his hands as well as his brain is better fitted for life's struggles."[59] One can hypothesize that another factor may have prevented Negroes from becoming involved in the battle against the Cooley Bill. Organized labor led the opposition against the proposal, and Negroes felt no identity with the unions because unions were generally not open to them. Given organized labor's racial prejudices, it would be unlikely that blacks would support an effort closely identified with such a group. Whatever the cause, Negroes did not take part in one of the most impassioned public debates on the consequences of the differentiated curriculum. From 1913 to 1917, the battle over the proposal continued, and, ultimately, the critics of the proposal were victorious. Vocational education and the classical academic curriculum would remain in a comprehensive high school under a single administrative structure. Hence, children in Chicago continued, at least theoretically, to have latitude in the upper grades in choosing their courses of study.

In cities throughout the nation which were revamping their curricula, the vocational education program, the two-year commercial courses, and the industrial and household arts curricula established a ceiling on social mobility for all children enrolled in them.[60] For Negroes, it was simply one more restriction operating in an environment which for them was fraught with discouraging barriers. While limited opportunity within the larger society and within the schools destroyed the aspirations and initiative of many young blacks, it did not crush the educational and occupational goals of all of them. It was this phenomenon which many educators, particularly vocational counselors, were amazed to encounter when they dealt with Negro students. Yet, rather than foster and reinforce these students' goals, they frequently complained of the Negroes' unrealistic aims and attempted to guide them into areas of training and employment where large numbers of their brothers and sisters were already located. Perhaps none of the educational reforms of the period provides as much evidence for the lack of provision in the modern school system for significant upward mobility for Negroes as the field of guidance counseling.

Coupled with the rise of curriculum expansion and variation and the introduction of junior high schools, guidance counseling emerged as part of the schools' services, generally at the level above the sixth grade. Guidance counseling was praised as one more means of dealing with the varying needs, concerns, and ultimate career decisions of the individual child. Counseling quickly became linked with the other reforms of the 1920s, the use of intelligence tests and ability groupings. A *Research Bulletin* of the Chicago Board of Education published in the mid-1920s discussed the relationship. In the section related to vocational guidance, the *Bulletin* stated that the results of the army intelligence tests indicated that "the amount of mental ability required for the various occupations, highest to lowest, is as follows: Professional and business, clerical, skilled trades, semi-skilled trades, unskilled labor." The report admitted that there was "considerable overlapping in the general ability of workers engaged in these occupations, yet there is a distinct difference in the general mental level of the groups."[61] In other words, a basic premise of vocational counseling as well as intelligence testing was that intelligence quotient scores matched the social order of the larger society. Some Philadelphia schoolmen operated on similar assumptions. One educator involved with Negro schools in the city wrote approvingly that research "suggests that the occupational status of the parents of Negro children is a fairly safe index of the mentality and achievement that are to be expected from them."[62] As one critic indignantly noted about this belief, "It is as though the relative social positions of each group are determined by an irresistible natural law."[63] The *Bulletin* went on to assert that the intelligence test results of pupils in the Chicago high schools demonstrated that "the pupils of higher mental ability select the more difficult courses in school, where the pupils of lower mental ability select the technical and commercial courses, and those selecting the two year vocational course show lowest ability."[64] The critics of intelligence testing scoffed at this evidence and argued that the choice of courses was determined to a much greater extent by the social and economic status of the pupil than by intelligence ranking. Children whose families needed additional income in order to survive in the city would likely select a two-year commercial or industrial course rather than a four-year academic program.[65]

Educators throughout the country echoed the beliefs stated in the Chicago publication. As Chapter 3 indicates, they viewed the social order as based on a meritocracy in which intelligence scores correlated reliably with present and future status in life. According to this view, it was the role of the vocational counselor to channel and direct students into appropriate programs. Vocational education was thus, according to counselors, the obvious curriculum for most lower class black students who had few books at home, no piano, often no indoor plumbing, and parents who had gone only through grade school.[66]

Vocational training or the commercial course might have been appropriate for some Negro students, just as it might have been for some whites. But protests rising from black communities suggest that some guidance counselors recommended such a curriculum for virtually all Negro students. In 1930, the Senior High Girl Reserves of a Negro branch of the Philadelphia YWCA chose for their monthly discussion topic, "Race Prejudice in the Philadelphia High School—Whose Fault?" In the discussions, the girls charged that they were urged to take home economics and nursing courses, regardless of their personal choice or ability. Other black students who wanted to be teachers alleged that guidance counselors had recommended they attend the Negro state normal school.[67] One black mother and former teacher in the Philadelphia schools recalled that her son, who attended a mixed school in the city during this period, planned to go to college. Nevertheless, school advisors urged him to take the auto mechanics curriculum in high school.[68]

In his autobiography, Malcolm X reported his experience of discussing his vocational plans with one of his high school teachers in Lansing, Michigan. He was one of the best students in his school, but when he said he was thinking about becoming a lawyer, the teacher was surprised. The man replied, "Malcolm, one of life's first needs is for us to be realistic." He continued, "A lawyer—that's no realistic goal for a nigger." He then suggested that because Malcolm "was good with his hands," carpentry would be appropriate for him.[69]

Such an experience was not unusual, and many counselors who urged their Negro students to go into vocational education based their advice not so much on racial prejudice as on educators' views of the role of the school vis-à-vis the social order. In their view, the schools should not or

could not be used as levers for social change. Instead, they should incul-
cate and perpetuate the values of the status quo. This meant they should
teach Negro students to be "realistic" about their chances in the world
of employment.

This tendency of guidance programs to maintain and perpetuate the
prevailing values of society received documentation in a doctoral dissertation by Virginia Daniels at the University of Pittsburgh in 1938. No evidence exists to suggest that a decade earlier guidance policies related to
Negroes were noticeably different from those she encountered. The doctoral
student sent questionnaires to guidance counselors throughout the North.
After compiling the responses, she concluded that the "attitudes of the
Negro students and the guidance officers seem to be the direct result of
the existing social order." She also indicated the guidance policy for
Negroes in northern schools as "more of an evasion rather than an attempted
solution of the problem.[70]

Not all guidance counselors followed the policy of discouraging Negro
students from ambitious career goals. For example, to the question
"Should Negro students prepare for their desired field or for work likely
to be open?," one Chicago vocational counselor replied, "Negroes must
enter lines of work which are open in order to live, but if they are coun-
selled to stay where they are, we enter an undemocratic procedure of
counselling. . . . We would thus perpetuate a condition of inequality
of opportunity for American citizens."[71]

According to Daniels' survey, it seemed that in theory the vast majority
of counselors adhered to the belief that Negro pupils should be counseled
to prepare and to seek to enter lines of work which were in accordance
with their interests and ambitions. Yet, to the question "Should they be
counseled merely to enter those lines of work in which there is reasonable
expectancy of obtaining employment?" 29.6 percent answered yes, 34.6
percent responded no, and 35.8 percent were undecided.[72]

Guidance personnel exhibited a similar ambivalence on the issue of increased job opportunities for Negroes. On the one hand, 73 percent believed that Negroes should have a wider range of occupational opportunities; on the other hand, only 34 percent believed that Negroes should be
encouraged to organize their power as consumers in order to force occupational openings from white-owned businesses which depended on Negro
buyers.[73] The job ceiling which Negroes faced and which dismayed many
educators would not be attacked by any power the schools might have,

nor would most schoolmen encourage active mobilization of any potential power the black community might have to affect it.

Despite the job restrictions and the school people's frequent encouragement of Negro students to pursue a vocational program, many blacks shied away from such a curriculum. The Chicago Commission on Race Relations discovered that Negro children preferred the academic program to the trade curriculum. Teachers and principals cited "the better social standing" which these academic courses would provide as the reason for their choice. One principal claimed that "Negroes want to know nothing about industrial training" and that "the girls don't care for sewing and cooking."[74] In a Chicago survey of Negro boys and girls about to enter high school whose fathers were unskilled laborers, factory workers, or janitors, 38 percent wanted to go into one of the professional fields and the majority of the others aspired to other white-collar jobs.[75] A counselor who had worked with Negro pupils in Philadelphia also discovered that a high percentage of Negro students aspired to white-collar jobs.[76] The stigma attached to vocational education programs was obvious to both students and schoolmen.

The stigma attached to black students was even more obvious to educators and pupils—and far more crucial. Yet, the educational reforms of the period did little to modify the prevailing racial prejudices. Rather, they provided a somewhat debatable scientific foundation for the image of Negro students as mentally inferior, low achievers, and candidates for diluted academic or industrial arts curricula. The schools assumed the role of labeling and educating these children accordingly and preparing them for their appropriate role in society. Certainly, the reformers did not introduce all the curricular revisions to subordinate the Negro; they frequently envisioned these programs as means of social uplift. But the consequences of these reforms did little to attack or threaten the entrenched prejudices of American society. Instead, they served a vital institution which helped perpetuate the Negro's substandard position in America.

NOTES

1. John and Evelyn Dewey, *Schools of Tomorrow*, pp. 150-166.

2. Ibid., p. 164.

3. Marvin Lazerson and W. Norton Grubb, eds., *American Education and Vocationalism: A Documentary History, 1870-1970*, Classics in Education, No. 48 (New York: Teachers College Press, 1974), pp. 24-25.

4. Charles W. Eliot, "Educational Reform and the Social Order," *School Review* 17 (April 1909): 217-219.

5. Ellwood P. Cubberley, *Changing Conceptions of Education* (Boston: Houghton Mifflin Co., 1909), pp. 56-57.

6. Indianapolis Public Schools, *Annual Report*, 1908-1909, p. 199.

7. G. Stanley Hall, *Adolescence*, Vol. 2 (New York: D. Appleton, 1904), p. 510.

8. Sol Cohen, "The Industrial Education Movement, 1906-17," *American Quarterly* 20 (Spring 1968): 101.

9. Doxey A. Wilkerson, "The Negro in American Education," p. 49 (Manuscript material used in preparation of Gunnar Myrdal, *An American Dilemma*), Schomberg Collection, New York City Public Library.

10. McDougald, "School and Its Relation to the Vocational Life of the Negro," p. 219.

11. See Meier's discussion in *Negro Thought in America*, pp. 85-91.

12. Ibid., p. 89.

13. *Indianapolis Freeman*, June 29, 1901.

14. W.E.B. DuBois, "Education," *Crisis* 4 (June 1912): 74-75.

15. Michael B. Katz, "Comment on Urban Education Symposium," *History of Education Quarterly* 9 (Fall 1969): 327.

16. John and Evelyn Dewey, *Schools of Tomorrow*, p. 161.

17. Boyer, *Adjustment of a School to Individual and Community Needs*, p. 100.

18. Indianapolis Public Schools, *Annual Report*, 1916, p. 168.

19. James E. Russell, "The Trend in American Education," *Educational Review* 32 (November 1906): 39.

20. Philadelphia Public Schools, *Annual Report of the Superintendent of Public Schools*, 1907, p. 18.

21. Odum, "Negro Children in the Public Schools of Philadelphia," p. 208.

22. Byron A. Phillips, "Retardation in the Elementary Schools of Philadelphia," *Psychological Clinic* 6 (May 15, 1912): 121.

23. Frederick W. Spears, "The James Forten School: An Experiment in Social Regeneration Through Elementary Manual Training," paper presented to the Civic Club of Philadelphia, March 2, 1911, p. 2.

24. Ibid., p. 10.

25. Ibid., p. 11.

26. Matthew Anderson, "The Berean School of Philadelphia and the Industrial Efficiency of the Negro," *Annals of the American Academy of Political and Social Science* 33 (January 1909): 115.

27. Vincent P. Franklin, "Educating an Urban Black Community: The Case of Philadelphia, 1900-1950" (Ph.D. dissertation, University of Chicago, 1975), p. 242.

28. Wright, *Negro in Pennsylvania*, p. 190.

29. *Philadelphia Tribune*, August 28, 1915.

30. Ibid.

31. Ibid., July 10, 1915.

32. W.E.B. DuBois, "Education," *Crisis* 10 (July 1915): 136.

33. Pennsylvania State Department of Public Instruction, *Report of the Survey*, Book III, p. 295.

34. Ibid., Book II, p. 193.

35. Ibid., p. 187.

36. *Philadelphia Tribune*, October 27, 1972.

37. Indianapolis Public Schools, *Annual Report*, 1908-1909, p. 199.

38. Baker, *Following the Color Line*, p. 140.

39. Indianapolis Public Schools, *Annual Report*, 1916, p. 80.

40. Ibid., p. 77.

41. Ibid.

42. Ibid., p. 78.

43. DuBois, "Education," *Crisis* 4 (June 1912): 74-75. William Torrey Harris, U.S. commissioner of education from 1889 to 1906, maintained views similar to those of DuBois. He stressed the need for intellectual instruction for Negroes and contended that Negroes did not need training in the "habits of industry, for he has had this discipline for two hundred years." William Torrey Harris, "The Education of the Negro," *Atlantic Monthly* 69 (June 1892): 724.

44. Ibid., p. 75.

45. Ibid.

46. *Indianapolis Freeman*, October 21, 1899; June 8, 1901; March 18, 1905.

47. Ibid., October 23, 1909.

48. *Indianapolis News*, May 13, 1919.

49. George Hayes, "Vocational Education and the Negro," National Society for the Promotion of Industrial Education, *Bulletin No. 24* (1917): 73.

50. Indianapolis Board of School Commissioners, *Minutes*, November 24, 1914, Book R, p. 120.

51. W.E.B. DuBois, "The Common School," *Crisis* 16 (July 1918): 112.

52. Ibid.

53. Chicago Commission on Race Relations, *Negro in Chicago*, pp. 438-439.

54. *Chicago Defender*, February 26, 1916.

55. Mary Jo Herrick, *Chicago Schools: A Social and Political History* (Beverly Hills, Calif.: Sage Publishing Co., 1971), p. 177.

56. Counts, *School and Society in Chicago*, p. 139.

57. Ibid.

58. Michael Wallace Homel, "Negroes in the Chicago Public Schools, 1910-1941" (Ph.D. dissertation, University of Chicago, 1972), p. 154.

59. *Chicago Defender*, November 23, 1912.

60. One would not argue that a student taking such a curriculum might not experience mobility to a certain degree—that is, the individual's parents might be unskilled workers, while he or she might become a skilled laborer or domestic. However, the ceiling on the potential mobility would be lower than that possible for pupils graduating from an academic curriculum.

61. Chicago Board of Education, *Research Bulletin* No. 1, Bureau of Standards and Statistics, Division of Instructional Research, quoted in Counts, *School and Society in Chicago*, p. 186.

62. John Henry Brodhead, "Educational Achievement and Its Relation to the Socio-Economic Status of the Negro" (Ph.D. dissertation, Temple University, 1937), p. 24.

63. Counts, *School and Society in Chicago,* p. 186.

64. Ibid., p. 187.

65. Ibid.

66. See example of guidance questionnaire in Marechal-Neil E. Young, *Some Sociological Aspects of Vocational Guidance of Negro Children* (Philadelphia: By the Author, 1944), p. 6.

67. *Philadelphia Tribune,* March 6, 1930.

68. Interview with Mrs. Marion Minton at her home, Germantown, Pennsylvania, January 29, 1972.

69. Malcolm X, *The Autobiography of Malcolm X* (New York: Grove Press, 1966), p. 36.

70. Virginia Daniels, "Attitudes Affecting the Occupational Affiliation of Negroes" (Ph.D. dissertation, University of Pittsburgh, 1938), p. 88.

71. Ibid., p. 72.

72. Ibid., p. 67.

73. Ibid., p. 66.

74. Chicago Commission on Race Relations, *Negro in Chicago,* p. 269.

75. Letitia Fyffe Merrill, "Children's Choices of Occupations," *Chicago Schools Journal* 5 (December 1922): 157.

76. Young, *Some Sociological Aspects of Vocational Guidance,* p. iii.

5 THE EARLY YEARS: SEGREGATION BEFORE THE GREAT MIGRATION

Segregation has been the most obvious manifestation of racism in the education of the American Negro in the past hundred years. The inferior quality of most separate schools also served as the clearest indication of the black child's position in the northern educational system. Segregated schools were deeply rooted in the antebellum North, and assaults on the dual educational system produced only isolated victories before the 1870s and 1880s.[1] During these postwar decades, many northern states passed laws prohibiting segregation in the public schools. Nevertheless, the separate school remained a familiar institution in northern cities and towns.

Mixing of the races in the schools aroused white supremacists not only because it allowed social contact between blacks and whites but also because these opponents feared, according to Forrest Wood, "that children were too young to exercise mature judgment and might unwittingly embrace the idea of social equality."[2] The North as well as the South was unprepared for such equality in a period marked by scientific pronouncements of Negro inferiority, academicians' exaltation of Anglo-Saxon superiority, and the emasculation of the Fourteenth Amendment. Consequently, Negroes who anticipated the full freedom and opportunity promised in the civil rights laws experienced disappointment and discrimination in the schools as well as in every other area of northern society.

Educational segregation in the North during the early twentieth century took at least three forms, and Indianapolis, Philadelphia, and Chicago exemplify these three different policies of segregation. In Indianapolis, the least common form of racial separation in the North, de jure segregation, existed. An Indiana law enacted in 1877 allowed individual boards of education to determine whether mixed or separate schools for the races should be established in each town. This law marked a significant step forward for the state's blacks, since before this time no law required Indiana communities to provide for the education of Negro residents. Thus, in Indianapolis, school policy designed to separate the races was open and legal.

De facto segregation, however, produced many more separate schools in the North. In Philadelphia, schoolmen officially acknowledged and sanctioned de facto segregation. The Pennsylvania legislature had passed a law in 1881 forbidding any distinction in the admission of pupils to a school due to race or color. Philadelphia school officials chose to ignore this law and throughout the period designated official "colored schools" staffed by Negro teachers for many black pupils.

The most subtle form of de facto segregation—and the most difficult to pinpoint and combat—emerged in Chicago, where school officials neither officially sanctioned nor acknowledged separation of the races. In practice, however, school administrators introduced segregation devices such as the transfer system and the gerrymandering of school districts in order to circumvent the Illinois law of 1874 which prohibited officials from excluding any child from a school on the basis of race. These de facto segregation methods did not receive national condemnation until the 1960s when the federal government, prodded by the civil rights movement, charged numerous northern cities, including the three considered in this study, with discriminatory policies.

The separate school in the North was therefore not imported from the South nor was it introduced only after the Great Migration. Segregation burdened many black children of the early twentieth century, just as it weighs down their descendants in the contemporary ghetto school.

PHILADELPHIA

Since 1822, Philadelphia had committed itself to provide public education for its Afro-American children, but community prejudice blocked many Negroes when they attempted to register their children in white schools after the passage of the 1881 law. A letter to Jacob White, Jr., the leading Negro educator in Philadelphia and principal of the Robert

Vaux School, from an indignant parent in 1881 indicated a common experience of the city's blacks in the following decades. The mother informed Principal White that she was returning her child to White's colored school because she could not get her daughter admitted to a white school located near her home. She declared that "there is some humbugging about us sending our children to white schools, and if it is a law there should be something done as she has lost a great deal of time."[3] One woman who failed to get her children admitted to a white school "because they were too full" related to Principal White that the appearance of her family at the school "raised a great excitement among the children and teachers." Some of the pupils threatened to leave, others cried "Nigger," and one teacher directed the woman to take her children to a colored school.[4] In fact, the school might have been full, for principals had to turn away many students of all races from overcrowded schools during these years. The frequency with which schoolmen used this explanation to bar black students, however, made black parents understandably skeptical.

Members of both the white and black community were ambivalent about the desirability of desegregated schools. Some middle-class blacks supported segregated schools because they believed that the only opportunity for employment that Negro graduates of the normal school had was in segregated schools, since the board of education permitted no blacks to teach white children. By 1897, approximately forty Negroes held coveted teaching positions in the public schools. This number constituted only about 1.5 percent of the teaching force of the city.[5]

Philadelphia civic leaders, including the board of education, were sympathetic with the Negro community "supporting their own" by petitioning for separate schools. In 1896, the chairman of the Committee on Schools of the city council urged that more separate schools be established. Councilman M. E. Mehan cited the number of Negro normal school graduates who were unemployed because "it is taken for granted that only white teachers shall be placed in charge of white children."[6] The councilman recommended that the Negro graduates be appointed to schools "in the centre of some colored population, so that colored people might support their own teachers if so disposed, as they support their own ministers in their separate churches."[7] He went on to praise the good result of such an arrangement by pointing out the two schools with seven colored teachers in the Twenty-second Section which "ranked among the most popular in the section."[8]

The white community in Philadelphia was generally careful to couch their suggestions for segregated schools in terms of increased job opportunities or beneficial education policy for the Negroes. In 1897, the *Philadelphia Public Ledger* headlined one of its articles "Educators Recommend Separate Schools for Colored Youth." The white newspaper reported that the Committee of Fifteen of the National Education Association recommended the establishment of "distinctive schools for Negro youth" taught by Negro teachers. After commending the good records of the colored schools of Philadelphia, the reporter suggested that the segregation proposal be considered seriously. He hastened to point out, however, that the recommendation "must be looked at from the educational standpoint and not from the social, as on the latter grounds distinct schools could not for a moment either be upheld or tolerated."[9] He did not comment on the justification for the colored schools already functioning in Philadelphia.

Whatever the defense for segregation, 1,316 Negro students were attending the six segregated schools in the Philadelphia system in 1897. The other 4,946 black children in school were in mixed schools, although some of these were almost completely segregated.[10] One glaring example was the J. S. Ramsey School which was not designated a colored school and was staffed by white teachers; yet, only about six of approximately five hundred students were white.[11] Philadelphia Negroes, however, did not press for integration during the late nineteenth century or in the first years of the twentieth because the community was divided in sentiment and unorganized. Not until 1908 did Negroes actively protest and organize against segregation policy.

In 1907, Superintendent Martin Grove Brumbaugh devoted part of his annual report to "the problem of the colored child." He first observed that there were more colored children in Philadelphia schools than in any other school system in the nation. He acknowledged the existence of some separate schools and noted the jobs these schools provided for the Negro community. Another advantage of these schools, he asserted, was the opportunity for the colored child to progress at his own rate through the curriculum. In his opinion, the Negro student's rate of progress was somewhat different from the rate of other children. For these reasons, he proposed that "whenever possible separate schools should be inaugurated for the colored children."[12]

Brumbaugh admitted that the establishment of separate schools would have to "be conditioned upon the petition of the parents of the children themselves." He viewed the possibility of parents insisting that their children remain in the mixed schools as "a really difficult situation." For, he argued, "the fact is that when the percentage of colored children reaches thirty or more the other children begin gradually to withdraw from the school."[13] One solution the superintendent proposed was to establish colored divisions or separate classes for Negroes taught by black teachers in mixed schools. He observed that such a plan was in operation in the Mary Washington School and suggested that it might be extended to other areas of the city.[14] In order to ascertain the reaction of the Negro community to increased segregation, he wrote leading Negroes in Philadelphia to ask their opinion.

The black community was sharply divided in its response to Brumbaugh's proposal. One group, led by the Reverend William A. Creditt, whose members all had daughters who were normal school graduates, viewed Brumbaugh's recommendations as an opportunity to obtain more jobs for Negroes.[15] Creditt and others met with the board and petitioned for more segregated schools. Their immediate plea was for the administrators to designate the Pollock School as a colored school because 85 percent of its students were black. Their request was strengthened by a petition signed, according to Brumbaugh, by four hundred Negro parents who lived in the area surrounding the school. They asked that Pollock "be set apart."[16]

The superintendent and the section board moved quickly to segregate the classes at Pollock, and they hired eight Negroes to teach the black students in the school. Brumbaugh reported that the local district board gave the plan its "hearty approval."[17] The board promised that as soon as they could transfer the white children to another school, four more Negro teachers and a black supervising principal would join Pollock's staff. It appeared that Creditt's group had succeeded, but one result of this incident turned out to be most unfortunate in the long run for Negro teacher candidates. Using Creditt's petition as an indication of the Negroes' desire for more black teachers, even if it meant more segregation, Brumbaugh established a dual list of teacher applicants, one white and one Negro. This dual list remained in effect until 1937. Thus, a practice of never hiring Negro teachers for mixed classes hardened into official policy.

Further plans for the increase of officially sanctioned segregation were curtailed by the vigorous opposition of another part of the community.

Many Negroes, spurred on by the outspoken criticism of Brumbaugh and Creditt by the African Methodist *Christian Recorder,* strenuously objected to further segregation. The superintendent received numerous protests against his "Jim Crow" proposal, and the antisegregationists organized protest meetings. They warned Philadelphia Negroes that the ultimate result of allowing Brumbaugh to implement his proposals would be total segregation. The protesters argued that "they preferred less work for their children as teachers and more recognition as citizens."[18] The critics also prophesied that segregation would not be limited to elementary schools but would also expand to the high schools.

The opposition within the Negro community caused Brumbaugh to postpone the idea of establishing separate schools for Negro children. However, the superintendent did not dismiss the plan to separate Negro children from other pupils in the schools. Instead, segregation was implemented through less obvious ways such as transfers of most white children out of predominantly Negro schools and the establishment of separate classes in mixed schools for Afro-American students. Thus, by 1911, there were no more colored schools than the nine which existed after the Pollock School was added in 1908, despite requests from some blacks for more Negro schools.[19] About 24 percent of the Negro children were students in these schools, while the remaining three-fourths were enrolled in what were termed mixed schools. In fact, however, these schools were either almost all black or all white. Only 15 percent of the total schools in the city had any black students.[20] According to a special study made for the Philadelphia Bureau of Municipal Research in 1911, no Negroes attended 31 percent of the schools; 23 percent of the schools had less than 1 percent; and 20 percent of the schools had between 1 and 5 percent Negro enrollment.[21]

These figures point up not only the minimal mixing of the races in the schools, but also the few opportunities this system of technically mixed as well as segregated schools offered black teachers. For in no school in which even 1 percent of the pupils was white was a black teacher placed. Thus, little benefit accrued to the black community as far as increased jobs for Negro educators were concerned. At no time during the first three decades of the twentieth century did the black teaching force represent more than 3.2 percent of the city's teachers.[22]

The antisegregationists resumed active protest against the policy of the board of education toward Negro children in 1912, led now by the

Tribune. In a February editorial, this black newspaper urged the community to meet and organize immediately because "the general public ought to know that Superintendent Brumbaugh, aided by a few sly colored men, is determined to make the colored people of our city endure the objectionable [separate school] system."[23] The *Tribune* saw as ominous indications of the superintendent's plans the instructions given every colored teacher applying for a job. The applicant was told "to go around among her people and get together a group of children and the Superintendent of Education will do the rest."[24]

The *Tribune* continued to try to rouse public opinion against segregation in the following weeks, declaring "if we are to have public schools in Philadelphia, let us have public schools in fact. Open to the public, white and colored teachers and scholars alike."[25] "It is in the school room where children are educated either to despise colored people or respect them," the newspaper proclaimed. "The separate school house . . . gives children the wrong kind of education for future citizenship."[26]

Some blacks did organize and quietly began an investigation of administrative policy and school conditions. Nevertheless, public opinion was still split on the question of segregated schools, and lack of community cohesion as well as apathy were continual sources of frustration to the activists. The *Tribune* warned its readers that "our status in the school world is being daily assailed and restricted." Chastising Philadelphia Negroes for their failure to fight, the writer argued that "we sit supinely down [and] pat our feet." Concluding the plea for action, the *Tribune* exhorted the freemen, "Arouse and prove your worth."[27]

The citizens' committee did proceed with its investigation of the schools and in the summer released the results. It charged that, within Philadelphia, "two thousand colored American children of school age are discriminated against and segregated in the public schools."[28] Negro children, the committee stated, were not admitted in certain schools and were thus forced to walk long distances. In schools that were officially mixed, the investigators found that in some rooms Negro children were instructed to sit on one side of the room away from the white pupils. The committee report cited instances in which the black students attending an integrated school were placed in a separate room where several grades were taught by one teacher. Another segregation device which the administration used, according to the report, was to establish annexes to white schools which were "badly located, unsanitary, and overcrowded, while the parent building is large and well ventilated."[29] The committee discovered unoccupied rooms in the main building which they asserted were sufficient to accommodate the Negro children who were relegated to the annex. Alleviation of such conditions, the committee argued, lay in getting a Negro on the school board to serve as a watchdog against racial discrimination. The group threatened to go to court if their demand for an end to discrimination and their request for a black school board member went unheeded. The person the committee proposed as best qualified to represent the race was Dr. N. F. Mosell, a prominent Philadelphia Negro. Such a man, they hoped, could block the "damning tide of race proscription which threatens to deluge the entire school area."[30]

Fears of further school segregation increased when Chester, a town located near Philadelphia, expanded segregation in its schools in 1912. Concern was heightened when, shortly after Chester segregated all black elementary schoolchildren, one of the morning papers carried an editorial supporting Chester's policy and argued the need of segregated schools in Philadelphia.[31] The *Tribune* struck back, denouncing the segregationists and their view that "the school house is the backbone of democracy— for everybody but the black child." The black newspaper condemned "the bait of a few jobs" by the "Machiavellian separatists" and denounced those Negroes "who did not consider the greatest good for the greatest number."[32]

Black students experienced segregation not only at the elementary school level but also in some high school activities. For example, in 1915 white pupils enrolled in physical education at the West Philadelphia High School for Boys received eighty minutes of swimming instruction each week at the West Branch YMCA. The instructor directed Negro students in the same course to remain at the school during this period. He told them that if they wanted to swim, they could go to the black YMCA once a week and take a "free swim" without instruction. Only after a black parent lodged numerous protests did the school send the swimming instructor to the black YMCA at a specific hour each week to teach the Negro students.[33]

Despite the black community's knowledge of the discrimination and segregation which existed in the schools, no protest movement received complete support from Philadelphia Negroes during these years of increasing separation of the races. They brought no court case and developed no sustained pressure for a black representative on the board. Thus, Brumbaugh and the school board, recognizing this lack of unity, chose to ignore the protests and did not support the appointment of a Negro to the policy-making body. By World War I, Philadelphia Negroes, despite the fact that their children made up over 5 percent of the 200,000 clients of the city schools, remained powerless and divided. Caught in the dilemma of the attraction of more jobs through segregation or greater equality of education through integration, they failed to realize the full benefit of either alternative. They were therefore unable to effectively combat policies which the schools introduced during the war years to isolate their children and the increasing number of Negro migrants who filled the schools.

INDIANAPOLIS

Like Philadelphia, Indianapolis maintained separate as well as mixed schools. In Indiana, separate schools were not illegal because of the option provided local boards of education in the 1877 law. Although Indianapolis chose not to officially ban Negro children from the white schools after 1878, almost all of the 1,113 Negro children in the schools in 1879 continued to attend one of the four colored elementary schools.[34] At the high school level there was no segregation, for the few Negroes in high school attended the only high school in the city. As early as 1872, the superintendent, A. C. Shortridge, had admitted Negroes to the high school rather than establish a separate school or prohibit the black students from obtaining high school training. Shortridge instituted this policy without consulting the board of school commissioners. One of the commissioners soon confronted the superintendent with the accusation, "I understand you have a nigger in the high school."[35] The superintendent held firm, the precedent was established, and the question of segregating high school students did not arise again until the years immediately before World War I. Although by 1887 only nineteen Negroes had graduated from the high school, the number of Negroes going beyond grammar school was increasing, and in 1896 six midyear graduates were black.[36]

From the time the board established mixed schools until World War I, little organized protest arose from the less than agressive black community about the fact that almost all of their children remained in segregated schools. A few individuals, however, did object to the barriers which many white principals erected around their schools to avoid admission of black students. In 1894, a Negro parent, Benjamin T. Thornton, resisted the order by the superintendent to transfer his daughter along with other Negroes from a predominantly white school to a segregated one. The superintendent had directed the black children to attend the colored school which was located further from their homes because of the crowded conditions in the white school. Thornton refused and took his child back to the school she had attended and commanded her, "Take your seat." He argued that it was unfair to make his child walk further to school, and he added: "Children can't get any kind of education at the colored schools. The principal of the colored school hasn't got as good an education as I have."[37]

Some Negroes met to discuss the superintendent's action and decried the effort being made "to draw the color line," but the protest was not sustained.[38] The Negro principal of the school to which the children transferred blunted the protest to some extent. He argued that "it was right for colored children to be taken out of white schools to make room for the white children when there was room in the colored schools." He also tried to refute the contention that the colored school was inferior by pointing out that the assistant superintendent in charge of elementary schools, Miss Nebraska Cropsey, believed that "the quality of education in the segregated schools was as high as in any other school in the city."[39]

The Negro community revealed further disagreement as to the justification of the superintendent's directive when four black citizens submitted a petition to the board of school commissioners. They wrote that "our colored children will fare as well under the instruction of our colored teachers, other things being equal, as they would under the instruction of a white teacher."[40] The petitioners informed the school commissioners that they did not approve of their children attending "schools set apart for white children when they can be accommodated in the colored schools."[41]

Thornton persisted in his opposition to the transfer by taking the case to court. He was defeated when a municipal judge ruled that the Negro student must attend a colored school if so ordered by the board of school commissioners.[42] This decision was a blow to parents who hoped to obtain more integration, and although mixed schools continued, only a few black pupils were involved.

No further protests concerning the segregation policy arose for a number of years, but frequently black delegations would petition for better school facilities for their children.[43] Many of the Negroes seemed satisfied with the arrangement and pointed with pride to the number of Negro teachers in Indianapolis, which by 1909 numbered 62 out of a total of 869 teachers.[44]

One black leader dissatisfied with the lack of integration was Gabriel Jones, a representative in the general assembly from Indianapolis. He introduced a bill in 1898 to end segregated schools in the state because, he argued, Negro schools were inferior to the white schools and should not be maintained. The bill passed the lower house but encountered serious opposition in the upper house. The legislators turned to George L. Knox, editor of the influential Negro newspaper of Indianapolis, the *Freeman*, to ask his opinion about the bill. Knox recommended that the legislators vote against the bill to abolish separate schools because of the loss of jobs for Negro teachers that would result. The bill was defeated, and no public outcry from Indianapolis blacks followed.[45]

Even a small percentage of Negroes in mixed schools produced distress among some school officials. In 1909, 2,330 Negroes were enrolled in the school system. All but fifty of the children below the high school level attended one of the segregated schools, while about eighty Negroes attended each of the two high schools.[46] The superintendent, G. N. Kendall, saw even this number of Negro students in classes with white pupils as objectionable. In a memorandum to the board of school commissioners in 1908, he observed that "the question of colored children attending white schools is becoming constantly more serious." The number of blacks in the high schools concerned him most, and he suggested in the memorandum that "the board should look forward to providing separate accommodations for colored high school pupils." Prophetically, he concluded that "sooner or later it will be necessary to remove the colored children from the high schools."[47] This memorandum was not publicized because, as Kendall reminded the commissioners, "it requires the greatest amount of diplomacy in this office and on the part of the principals to prevent an outbreak concerning this delicate question."[48]

The presence of Negro students in the high schools had caused relatively little friction through the years. In 1903, a white graduate of the Manual Training High School refused to sit by a Negro at commencement and was therefore not allowed to receive his diploma at the graduation exercises.[49] The *Freeman*, appalled at the incident, reported, "It is the first time such a happening has occurred in the schools of Indianapolis." The paper noted that "colored pupils had been receiving diplomas right beside

white pupils for a number of years," and there had been no distinction
at the school because "colored boys have been given the same chance on
the athletic teams of the schools as white boys."[50]

At graduation the next year, the paper reported no similar incident because the principal asked for volunteers to sit beside Negro graduates.
The boys who volunteered said they would sit beside Negroes because
"they regarded colored boys and girls who were equals in their studies
. . . [as] justly entitled to respect and credit."[51] The *Freeman* termed the
volunteers' decision "an act of heroism."[52]

The only other reported incident occurred in 1904 at Shortridge High
School, where a boy was suspended because he refused to sit next to a
Negro girl. The boy declared that he was assigned the seat as "punish-
ment." The school went into an uproar as a result of the suspension, but
Superintendent Kendall upheld the decision not to allow the student to
return to school until he apologized to the teacher.[53]

The continued failure of the Indianapolis Negro community to demand
its rights angered more militant Negroes in other cities. After visiting the
city, Monroe Trotter, editor of *The Boston Guardian*, urged Indianapolis
blacks to "heartily unite to put an end to the disgraceful denial of ordinary
civil rights and begin a stubborn fight to defeat this victory of the Bourbon
South in robbing them of their equality."[54] The *Freeman*'s response to
Trotter reflected the general stance of the community: "There is no reason
for a special campaign at this time . . . because we are accorded just about
the same consideration as we find accorded us under the most favorable
circumstances."[55] The editorial acknowledged that the condition was
"nothing to boast of," but "while restricted we are not inconvenienced.
Practically, or in some form, we have every right that can come to an
American citizen."[56]

A few months later, the same newspaper reflected a similar acquiescence
when it discussed Indianapolis school segregation. A reader asked that the
editor comment on a move to segregate all Negro students in Topeka,
Kansas, which the Negroes of Topeka supported. The editor pointed out
that while completely integrated schools were "ideal," conditions had
not yet reached that level. Negroes still faced separation and disrespect
in American society. The Negro should therefore attempt to develop
"community spirit" and support Negro teachers even if it meant separate
schools. "In view of the general separation the separate schools are mis-
sionary to a great extent," asserted the *Freeman*. Citing the experience

in Indianapolis, the editor praised the city's colored teachers because
"they do much in keeping alive an aggressive and helpful community
spirit . . . which could not be so great . . . under any other situation."[57]
A source of pride to the community was the record of Negro students
educated in the separate elementary schools as well as the performance of the black students who went on to one of the two mixed high
schools. "We set this [record] as an example of what separate schools
can do at their best, and which recommend them in view of the general
separate condition."[58]

Touching on the connection of separate schools and Negro employment, the *Freeman* argued that "employment of any kind is valuable to
the race, and since it is not found possible to enjoy much of it teaching
white children, it is best to get as much of it as possible teaching our own
children."[59]

It was not surprising, then, that the postwar period brought a more
active policy of school segregation to Indianapolis. School officials saw
the increasing number of Negro students in the mixed schools as a condition which must be remedied, and they believed that they could count
on the majority of the Negro community for support of or at least acquies-
cense to the increased segregation.

CHICAGO

In contrast to the response in Indianapolis, Negroes in Chicago demonstrated active opposition to any efforts throughout the period to establish
what they termed "Jim Crow schools." Some reports from Negroes attending the Chicago schools before 1900 suggested that educators made little
conscious effort to segregate the races in the schools, although school administrators commonly granted transfers for white children in predominantly
Negro school districts. In 1890, the Negro community made up only 1.3
percent of Chicago's population, and one black remarked that Negro
students were so scattered throughout the school system that to have
considered Negro education separately would have been an artificial
delineation.[60]

Between 1890 and 1900, the Negro population increased by 111 percent, while the total population rose only 54 percent. Negroes were becoming more visible, and in the first years of the century the number of
black enclaves was increasing.[61] Between 1900 and 1916, the hardening

line of white opposition to the influx of Negroes and the growth of the
ghetto made the issue of segregated schools a frequent threat to the black
community. In 1903, some of the leading Chicago Negroes organized the
Equal Opportunity League in order to work against the efforts of some
Chicagoans to impose segregation of Afro-American children in the schools.
The league was anxious to make public "a strong protest" and thereby
"forestall any move in that direction by the school board."[62]

The Equal Opportunity League failed to maintain support and by
1905 was defunct.[63] Two of its members, Charles Bentley and James
Madden, tried to resurrect an integrationist pressure group in 1905 when
they established an Illinois branch of the Niagara Movement. The threat
of school segregation in Chicago was one of its prime concerns. The following year the group succeeded in getting a Negro appointed to the New
Chicago Charter Commission in order to prevent acceptance of a rumored
clause in the charter which allowed segregated schools. The clause was not
incorporated in the charter, but proposals for segregated schools continued
to plague the black community.[64]

By 1906, the residential segregation pattern and the growing enrollment of Negro students caused one observer to exclaim, "There is not a
school east of State Street that is not complaining of the crowding of
Afro-American children."[65] The reporter was astonished that "the number [of black schoolchildren] is so large in some of the schools as to leave
the impression of separate schools."[66] The Black Belt south of the Loop
spread into residential areas which previously had no Negroes, and the
black children were enrolling in the neighborhood schools. One writer
noted that "some of these schools that formerly had not a single Afro-
American now have from five to one hundred at least."[67]

Friction between students often followed the Negroes' entrance into a
school. In 1902, the *Inter-Ocean* reported that two policemen were on
duty at the Farren School because of a "race riot" among the students.[68]
The same paper related in 1905 that the principal of the Tilden School
had summoned the police in order to avoid a riot between white and
Negro pupils. Tension between the groups had arisen the preceding week
when a Negro boy struck a white girl.[69] In 1907, nearly 250 white and
black students confronted each other with stones, clubs, and hatpins at
the Copernicus School in what the *Chicago Tribune* termed a "color
war."[70]

Often, as a school became predominantly black, the Negro children
themselves drew the color line against the white students. In the Keith

School in 1907, the Afro-American enrollment was more than twice as large as the white registration. Black pupils, according to one newspaper, "served notice on their white schoolmates that they are not wanted and that the sooner they get out the better."[71]

The transfer system was frequently used to bar black children from a white school or to allow white children to attend schools outside of heavily populated black areas. While this method was common in all three cities, in Chicago it became the most prevalent means of separating white and black pupils. In 1905, the *Chicago Tribune* stated that the requests of white pupils for transfers out of schools attended mainly by Negroes were unprecedented. The board of education initially granted these requests, but by December the shortage of space in schools outside the Black Belt led to discontinuation of the policy. Then, some of the white students who failed to obtain transfers became truants, while a few chose to go to the Parental School, a special school for children who chronically misbehaved, rather than to attend the school to which they were assigned.[72] School board members, confronted by irate white parents, decided to continue to grant wholesale transfers to white pupils but to refuse them to Negro students. One school board member commented that "ultimately other schools would have to be built just outside the 'black belt' to accommodate the white children transferred, but I believe this to be the only possible solution to the problem." He pointed out that East St. Louis had implemented such a plan with success.[73]

When questioned about the white demands for transfers, Superintendent Edwin G. Cooley declared that the schools faced "an unusually serious problem" concerning the racial friction. "Something must be done to prevent further trouble."[74] In later years, the superintendent and most of the board continued to be responsive to the demands from the white community to limit whenever possible the mixing of Negro and white children in the schools. In 1908, 150 white pupils who attended elementary school in the Lake High School building had to transfer to Hancock School because the space in the high school was needed. The Hancock School had a black enrollment of 10 percent, and the transferred children objected to attending class with the Negroes. Many of the white children who had come from Lake High School were from well-to-do families, and their parents immediately protested. A school strike followed in which most of the 150 transferred students remained out of school with parental approval. Alderman Michael McInerney headed a group which demanded a change in policy. McInerney declared to Cooley that the transfer was "a hardship that seems unjust to these pupils. They come from good families and they have been at a good building. Now they are told to go to an old building," he complained, "and to sit side by side with—well, with children they don't wish to sit beside."[75]

Although the board of education had originally stated that no room was available for the children in any other building, Cooley revoked the transfers after the protest. The white pupils either returned to the Lake High School building or transferred to a white elementary school. None had to remain at Hancock.[76]

The incident triggered complaints from parents and teachers in several other mixed schools about the problems which arose when Negro and white children attended the same school. When the president of the board, Otto C. Schneider, the only board member who was critical of the white demands for transfers, learned that teachers and parents of the Keith School were in favor of segregating the races in the schools, he termed the proposal "ridiculous." He asserted that "you can't segregate in the public schools. It's contrary to state laws. Think of having 'Jim Crow' schools in Chicago."[77]

Many Chicagoans, however, did not agree with President Schneider. The Hyde Park Improvement Protective Club, organized by residents trying to block the encroachment of Negroes into that residential area, actively supported segregated schools. In 1909, one club representative claimed, "It is only a question of time when there will be separate schools for Negroes throughout Illinois."[78]

By 1910, white protests occurred each time administrators drew new boundary lines which placed Negro and white children in the same classroom. Although rational use of school facilities was the primary basis on which schoolmen determined boundaries, the board on occasion altered boundary decisions because of pressure from white parents. This type of acquiescence by the board to white demands, Michael Homel has pointed out, probably encouraged and reinforced white opposition to integrated schools.[79]

Negro children who moved into an all-white school during these years of tension found the experience traumatic and lonely. In 1909, when the two children of a sleeping car porter registered at an all-white school, the attacks and insults from the other pupils were so intense that the principal had to act to protect the children. She instructed them to arrive at the school ten minutes after classes began in the morning, and she ordered teachers to dismiss them ten minutes early so they might be on their way home before the dismissal time of the other students.[80]

The middle class in the Negro community never supported segregated schools as a means of gaining more professional jobs, despite the fact that only sixty-four blacks in the city held teaching positions in 1910, a small number of which were in private schools. Negro teachers, who represented only 0.6 percent of Chicago's teaching force in that year, however, did hold a few positions in predominantly white schools.[81] In 1910, when the Southern Society of Chicago called for segregated schools in order to provide more employment for Negroes, middle-class indignation and counterattack were swift. According to the *Defender*, the society included southern whites and southern Negro migrants whom the outraged newspaper denounced as "southern white folks' lovers."[82] The group circulated petitions for separate schools in Chicago and argued that segregation would not only provide more jobs, but it would also enable Negro pupils to attend school "without fights and without having white folks calling them names."[83] The response to the society's petitions was only slight.

The *Defender*, which was irrevocably committed to integrated schools, countered the arguments of the Southern Society by publishing a picture of a mixed school class. According to the paper, the picture illustrated how well the children mixed because the colored children could be found "at every angle of the picture."[84] The militant paper proclaimed that it was "proud of Chicago's mixed schools"; furthermore, "We who live in Chicago would not . . . like having the added expense of having 500 schools added to our tax list . . . or getting the old stoves used by the whites."[85]

The militant crusade of the *Defender* and the opposition of the Negro community to segregation proposals ended any efforts among blacks to promote separate schools. This united resistance did not, however, deter various white groups. The most vigorous support of segregation in the schools continued to come from the Hyde Park Improvement Protective Club. In 1912, the organization petitioned the mayor to consider segregating the schools. H. T. Davis, president of the club, argued that "it would be better for the negroes themselves if the children were kept separate." He added that where there were only a few blacks in a school, "they are often abused by the whites and it would be a protection for them if they were kept by themselves."[86]

Negroes retaliated with protest meetings at which prominent blacks denounced the action, and letters poured into the mayor's office from Negroes protesting "Jim Crow" school proposals. The mayor ignored the Hyde Park Club's petition, but the group continued its efforts to segregate the school system. One vocal and powerful critic of segregation efforts was Mrs. Ella Flagg Young, who became superintendent of the Chicago schools in 1909. Mrs. Young, a former colleague of John Dewey at the University of Chicago and well-known Progressive in her own right, assailed the proposals for separate schools in Chicago and other metropolitan areas. "You people," she informed Washington, D.C., schoolmen after visiting their segregated schools, "are making a grave mistake to try to keep the colored people down." She proclaimed, "I for one will contend that all our countrymen should be taught in one school and we will find in the long run our nation will be richer by many millions."[87] She pointed out to the Washington educators that, in Chicago, "we have mixed schools, and we are proud of them. We have colored teachers, too, and we are proud of them, and to speak of the kindly feeling between them cannot be put too strongly."[88]

In many cases, the "kindly feeling" Mrs. Young referred to did not extend to white parents' attitudes about mixed schools. In 1915, she complained that social and racial distinctions in the schools disturbed her. "First it was the question of fraternities and sororities, and now it's the school permits." She lamented that "more than 94 per cent of requests by parents and children for permission to move from one school to another would carry the boy or girl into one of four schools," all of which had almost no black students.[89]

Even during Mrs. Young's superintendency, individual educators and board of education bureaucrats effected policies which discriminated or partially segregated black children. Negroes learned that, despite the existence of a fairminded superintendent, they had to remain wary and vigilant. When, in 1913, the school officials altered the boundaries of two schools on the South Side in such a way that one predominantly white and one predominantly black school resulted, Negroes became aroused. Black parents argued that the new districting meant that some of their children who lived 350 feet from a school had to walk a number of blocks to another school rather than attend the one nearest them. In this case, white children were also inconvenienced, and some of their parents also joined the protest. Negroes were uncertain whether the districting was the result of "the pernicious influence" of the Hyde Park Improvement Protective Club or "a prejudiced school official," but they were determined to contest the action.[90] The community was becoming increasingly aware that segregation could result from the less direct and obvious means of gerrymandering and wholesale transfers.

Negroes were also correct in scrutinizing the actions of schoolmen within individual schools. By 1914, Negroes were so concerned about "conditions of racial prejudice" in three high schools—Wendell Phillips, Hyde Park, and Englewood—that the NAACP branch in Chicago created a new Committee on Education.[91] Complaints related to policies at Wendell Phillips High School had arisen for several years as the school's black population steadily rose to nearly 20 percent of the student body. Five cases which related to discrimination at Wendell Phillips Night School came to the attention of the NAACP committee in 1914. The committee notified Superintendent Young of the complaints, and the discriminatory policies in the night school ceased.[92] It was not until 1915 that an incident occurred which enraged both black students and parents and caused the superintendent to intervene. One of the most outspoken segregationists was the dean of social activities, Miss Fannie Smith. In 1913, the *Defender* had accused her of supporting segregation and had reported that she had called a special meeting of Negro students to lecture them on the desirability of segregated schools.[93] Two years later, she arranged special social gatherings once a week rather than continuing the all-school parties. The black students refused to attend the segregated social affairs, and parents inundated the school with complaints. Miss Smith responded to the protests by stating that she believed "the Afro-American children could enjoy themselves much better if they were by themselves, that the white pupils would not come and that would mar the social side of school life."[94] After hearing of a complaint from the dean of women of the University of Chicago about the policy, she had justified her actions by explaining that some of the white pupils were from wealthy families in Kenwood and the parents did not like to see their children associating with colored pupils.[95]

When Superintendent Young met with an irate black delegation to discuss the segregated social affairs, Miss Smith announced that she intended to abolish the social hours. Instead, the school would hold intellectual-social hours which would include all students. Lectures, stereopticon shows, and debates on current topics replaced dancing. "When the children are in the classroom and at work or associated together in intellectual pursuits," she observed, "race distinction is never thought of. It was only when they were together on a purely social basis that difficulty came."[96] The *Defender* applauded her program and viewed the change as "a victory for racial equality."[97]

By 1915, Chicago's black leaders could view their efforts to maintain

integrated schools with a certain satisfaction. They had counteracted the
increasing sentiment for segregation among large numbers of whites on
the South Side by presenting a solid and alert front. Unlike Indianapolis
and Philadelphia, little ambivalence existed concerning the desirability
of mixed schools, even if separate schools would have provided more jobs
for their race. Yet, the achievements were offset to a significant extent
by the Negroes' lack of power to block the existence of de facto segregation produced not only by residential restrictions, but also by the practice
of granting transfers to white children living in mixed neighborhoods.
Furthermore, the growing number of blacks settling in Chicago and the
expanding ghetto had produced greater racial prejudice among white
citizens and no longer made the presence of black children in the city's
classrooms a minor issue. Hence, blacks who were concerned with quality
integrated education for their children viewed the spiralling number of
black migrants with concern as well as pride because the increase would
make more segregation attempts and further racial prejudice in the schools
a continual threat.

The years following the Great Migration of 1916 did confirm the fears
of older residents about intensified racial discrimination in all three cities.
Yet, the devices of segregation and the pattern of response of the educational systems in the North to the Negro in the postwar period were not
altered but followed those established in the early years of the century.
In the years since the white schools opened their doors to the black child,
schoolmen had developed policies of maintaining numerous de facto
segregated schools through the use of transfers, gerrymandering of districts, and separate classes for Negro students in mixed schools. Although
many children were students in separate schools in the North, it was
characteristic of these systems that segregation—even in Indianapolis during these years—was not absolute. As one contemporary educator remarked
concerning the pattern of northern segregation, "There is always a relatively small number of exceptions to the pattern of racial separation."[98]
The precedent was also established that those schools which were either
segregated or attended primarily by black students would be unequal in
quality. The inequality would become even more obvious in the following
years.
Common characteristics marked the high schools' policies toward
Negroes. The number of black students reaching high school during these
years was so small that administrators and the white community did not

impose separation of the races at this level, except in social activities and certain athletic programs in the school. Furthermore, the more prestigious high school posts which paid more than elementary school jobs were closed to all black teachers in these cities before World War I.

The small black middle class, the only group within the Negro community capable of spearheading protests against segregation and organizing the disparate groups, was often painfully torn on the one hand by the desire for job opportunities through separate schools and on the other by greater equality of education through integrated schools. This dilemma, compounded by the chronic lack of unity, made the Negro protest voice on educational issues weak and often impotent. Thus, either official or unofficial segregation and discrimination characterized the educational systems of these three cities as well as many other metropolitan areas in the North in the early twentieth century.

NOTES

1. For a description of black education in the North before the Civil War, see Litwack, *North of Slavery.*

2. Wood, *Black Scare,* p. 137.

3. C. Richards to Jacob C. White, Jr., October 12, 1881, Pennsylvania Historical Society, Jacob C. White, Jr., Papers.

4. Merle Nichols to Jacob C. White, Jr., September 5, 1881, Pennsylvania Historical Society, Jacob C. White, Jr., Papers.

5. DuBois, *Philadelphia Negro,* p. 113; MacLean, "Evolution of the Philadelphia School System," p. 157.

6. *Philadelphia Public Ledger,* December 2, 1896.

7. Ibid.

8. Ibid.

9. *Philadelphia Public Ledger,* August 13, 1897.

10. DuBois, *Philadelphia Negro,* p. 89.

11. *Philadelphia Public Ledger,* August 13, 1897.

12. Philadelphia Public Schools, *Annual Report of the Superintendent of Schools,* 1907, p. 17.

13. Ibid.

14. Ibid.

15. John A. Saunders, *One Hundred Years After Emancipation: History of the Philadelphia Negro, 1787-1963* (Philadelphia: *Philadelphia Tribune,* 1963), p. 186.

16. *New York Age,* November 5, 1908.

17. Ibid.

18. Ibid.

19. Philadelphia Board of Public Education, *Journal,* 1910, p. 264.

20. Odum, "Negro Children in the Public Schools of Philadelphia," p. 187.

21. Ibid.

22. Nelson, "Race and Class Consciousness of Philadelphia Negroes," p. 159.

23. *Philadelphia Tribune,* February 17, 1912.

24. Ibid.

25. *Philadelphia Tribune,* February 24, 1912.

26. Ibid.

27. *Philadelphia Tribune,* May 4, 1912.

28. *Crisis* 4 (July 1912): 111.

29. Ibid.

30. Ibid.

31. *Philadelphia Tribune,* September 28, 1912.

32. Ibid.

33. *Philadelphia Tribune,* November 13, 1915.

34. Indianapolis Public Schools, *Superintendent's Annual Report,* 1879, p. 74.

35. A. C. Shortridge, "The Schools of Indianapolis," *Indiana Magazine of History* 8 (June 1912): 128.

36. Thornbrough, *Negro in Indiana,* p. 341.

37. *Indianapolis Freeman,* September 29, 1894.

38. Ibid.

39. Ibid.

40. Indianapolis Board of School Commissioners, *Minutes,* May 3, 1895, Book I, p. 289.

41. Ibid.

42. Thornbrough, *Negro in Indiana,* p. 332.

43. Indianapolis Board of School Commissioners, *Minutes,* October 18, 1895, Book I, p. 363, Book O, October 12, 1909, p. 272.

44. Indianapolis Public Schools, *Superintendent's Annual Report,* 1908-1909, p. 24.

45. John W. Lyda, *The Negro in the History of Indiana* (Terre Haute: Indiana Negro History Society, 1953), p. 87.

46. Dunn, *Greater Indianapolis,* Vol. 1, p. 276.

47. Indianapolis Board of School Commissioners, *Minutes,* October 29, 1908, Book O, p. 77.

48. Ibid.

49. *Indianapolis Freeman,* June 13, 1903.

50. Ibid.

51. *Indianapolis Freeman,* June 4, 1904.

52. Ibid.

53. *Indianapolis Freeman,* March 12, 1904.

54. *Indianapolis Freeman,* April 10, 1915.

55. Ibid.

56. Ibid.

57. *Indianapolis Freeman,* June 26, 1915.

58. Ibid.

59. Ibid.

60. Report on Illinois education of Negroes in "The Negro in Illinois," a file of

reports and interviews compiled by the Illinois Writers Project of the Works Progress Administration (George Cleveland Hall Branch of the Chicago Public Library).

61. Spear, *Black Chicago*, p. 17.

62. *Broad-Ax*, December 19, 1903.

63. Spear, *Black Chicago*, p. 85.

64. Ibid., p. 86.

65. *New York Age*, September 20, 1906.

66. Ibid.

67. Ibid.

68. *Chicago Inter-Ocean*, November 14, 1902.

69. *Chicago Inter-Ocean*, November 29, 1905.

70. *Chicago Tribune*, December 5, 1905.

71. *New York Age*, October 10, 1907.

72. *Chicago Tribune*, September 25, 1908.

73. *Chicago Tribune*, September 19, 1908.

74. Ibid.

75. *Chicago Record-Herald*, October 10, 1909.

76. *Chicago Record-Herald*, November 11, 1909.

77. *Chicago Tribune*, September 29, 1908.

78. *Chicago Record-Herald*, October 10, 1909.

79. Homel, "Negroes in the Chicago Public Schools," pp. 50-51.

80. *Chicago Record-Herald*, November 11, 1909.

81. Spear, *Black Chicago*, pp. 30-31.

82. *Chicago Defender*, November 12, 1910.

83. Ibid.

84. Ibid.

85. Ibid.

86. *Chicago Defender*, February 14, 1912.

87. *Chicago Defender*, December 28, 1912.

88. Ibid.

89. *Chicago Defender*, February 6, 1915.

90. *Chicago Defender*, October 11, 1913.

91. *Chicago Defender*, March 21, 1914.

92. National Association for the Advancement of Colored People, *Fourth Annual Report*, p. 49.

93. *Chicago Defender*, November 1, 1913.

94. *Chicago Defender*, March 21, 1915.

95. *Chicago Herald*, January 9, 1915.

96. *Chicago Defender*, April 17, 1915.

97. Ibid.

98. Harold Baron, "Northern Segregation as a System: The Chicago Schools," *Integrated Education* 3 (December-January, 1965-1966): 55.

6 SEGREGATION AFTER THE GREAT MIGRATION

Beginning with the Civil War years, southern Negroes crossed the Mason-Dixon line in search of opportunity and equality. During World War I, the movement to northern cities accelerated to such an extent that this Great Migration became a major watershed in American black history.[1] Between 1916 and 1918, almost half a million Negroes deserted the South, most of them destined for urban centers such as Chicago, Philadelphia, New York, and Pittsburgh.[2]

Blacks abandoned their rural life for the beckoning cities for a number of reasons. The promise of jobs and higher wages in war-swollen industries lured many Negroes, weary of long hours of toil, defeated by the ravages of the boll weevil, and ground down by paltry incomes from sharecropping or tenant farming. Reports of less political and social repression in the North also motivated a people who were haunted by spectres of lynch mobs and were stripped of civil rights. Each letter from friends or family already in the North describing unbelievable salaries and urban opportunities encouraged migration. Each time a labor agent went south to recruit workers or an employment bureau advertised "thousand of jobs in the North," Negroes responded. Meagre belongings went into pillow cases or carpet sacks, and blacks boarded trains for the journey to the Promised Land.

Long-time Negro residents of northern cities watched with concern as their southern brothers and sisters streamed into the urban areas. Migrants were not welcomed with enthusiasm by many blacks or whites. The determination of whites that the newcomers should live only in black areas of the cities produced housing crises and overburdened Negro service and charity organizations. Even more significant, the migration brought the expansion of the ghettos and heightened residential segregation in many northern cities.[3] The spiralling black population triggered white resistance to all types of racial mixing, and more stringent segregation policies appeared throughout the cities which affected both old and new residents. One of the first institutions to reflect the increasing segregation and discrimination was the school.

PHILADELPHIA

The established black community in Philadelphia was perhaps more vociferous in its distaste for the newcomers than any other Negro urban group. These blacks lamented curtailment of admission to white restaurants, churches, and theatres. One former teacher and member of the Old Philadelphian black group herself, Mrs. Marion Minton, compared the type of Negro students one saw before the war with children from the South who poured into the schools during and directly after World War I. According to Mrs. Minton, the few who came in the early part of the century, even from southern states, were well disciplined and bright. Their parents valued education and supported the efforts of children in school. There were few problems with these students. With the influx of migrants in 1916 and subsequent years, however, she observed a different type of child appearing in the classroom. The new students were overage, often difficult to manage, and frequently caused trouble. The Old Philadelphians, Mrs. Minton recalled, resented them because more established Negro residents were anxious to raise the image of the black community.[4] One member of the Negro elite of the city erroneously claimed that Negroes previously "had always enjoyed the same social and educational facilities as the whites and courteous treatment from them. But with the increase in population by a group of generally uneducated and untrained persons, these privileges were withdrawn."[5]

One important result of the alienation of the older residents was an obvious lack of unity within the Negro community. Black Philadelphians were therefore placed at an even greater disadvantage in combatting growing segregation imposed by white-controlled institutions such as public education. Often, leaders of the black community channeled their resentment over loss of minimal acceptance by the white bourgeoisie into indignation toward migrants rather than toward white racists. Thus, the *Tribune* remonstrated with lower class Negroes for sending students to school untidy or unclean and declared that it was not unreasonable for people attempting to surround their families with good influences to be critical of their children sitting next to neglected, dirty pupils.[6]

Incidents of segregation were widespread in the schools, which were experiencing crowded classrooms, demands for special programs for the newly arrived southern child, and a marked increase in Negroes in the system. The number of black children in Philadelphia rose from 12,945 in 1915 to 16,682 in 1918, which was a rate of increase three times that of white students.[7] Administrators felt inundated by southern Negroes, and they placed as many of the new clients as possible in the existing separate schools. One black principal recalled cramped, gas-lit schoolrooms during the Great Migration years packed with sixty students per class ranging in age from eight to sixteen.[8]

The school system's desire to keep the races separated also affected Negro students at the University of Pennsylvania. Four black education majors at the university were not able to practice teach in the Philadelphia school system because administrators feared that some child might object to a Negro teacher.[9]

In 1917, a legislator introduced a bill in Harrisburg to segregate Negro and white students in public schools of the state. Although the author of the bill was an obscure legislator and it was unlikely that the bill would pass, the *Tribune* viewed the incident as one more ominous indication of rising sentiment for separate schools.[10] Among the forces outside the city which Negroes considered a threat to mixed schools was Governor Martin Grove Brumbaugh, former superintendent of Philadelphia schools and proponent of segregated educational facilities. Factors within the city which the *Tribune* warned Negroes to remain on guard against were white racist groups and also some black preachers and politicians who either benefited personally from segregation or were under the influence of "illiterate prejudiced white political leaders."[11] The paper reminded Negroes that "our experience is that the separately maintained colored schools . . . show the effects of the infernal prejudice of the white governing boards." Not only were buildings inferior but "courses were cut and surroundings were inferior."[12]

Educators frequently cited substandard performance and preparation by students from the South as reasons to provide separate schooling for

many Negroes. By 1920, one Philadelphia Negro who was principal of
an elementary school wrote the state superintendent of education about
his fear that the massive migration of rural southern blacks might "inspire
hostile and prejudicial sentiment which if unchecked, may develop into
reactionary, hasty, ill-judged action." He found that "evidences of this
hostility are appearing in many places."[13]

From the time of the Great Migration until a 1925 study was made,
no statistics are available on the extent of segregation in the schools.
By 1922, however, the local NAACP began to lodge frequent protests
with the board of education concerning "the progressive movement,
which is far along on its way, toward complete segregation of our colored
pupils, and colored teachers and principals in the public schools of Philadelphia."[14] Headed by the Presbyterian minister William Lloyd Imes, the
Committee on Public School Education and Race Relations of the NAACP
urged the board in 1922 to institute an inquiry into segregation policy
and compare Philadelphia's treatment of Negro students with that of
Chicago and New York.[15] The group also petitioned administrators to
institute an investigation of the cause of race antipathy and the best
means of alleviating prejudice. The committee suggested that the board
establish a mixed commission of white and Negro citizens, teachers,
school visitors, and parents to consider the problems.[16]

In July, the NAACP committee met with the board's subcommittee
on elementary schools and presented further proposals for halting the
increasing segregation. To reinforce their requests, the committee also
collected two thousand names of black citizens on a petition demanding
an end to school segregation. By December, the board had failed either
to respond or even reply to the group. Chairman Imes protested the
inaction. He reminded the educational policy-makers that the complaints
of Negro parents concerning conditions in one of the black elementary
schools had gone unnoticed. He cited not only the protests of Negro
citizens about the building but also those of a white resident of the area
who alleged that the school was rat infested, poorly lighted and ventilated,
and had poor sanitation and falling plaster.[17]

No recorded response by the board remains, and no measures were
taken to meet the demands of black citizens. In the past, Negro responses
to such inaction by the board were generally only halfhearted protest and
discontent, but by this time Philadelphia Negroes were beginning to exhibit
more militancy because of their concern about growing segregation through-

out the state. Black fears were fully justified since census data indicate that between 1920 and 1930 residential segregation in the city increased by over 35 percent.[18]

A second contributing factor to the new salience of the school issue was the editorial policy of the *Tribune*. Chris J. Perry, founder of the paper, died in 1921, and his son-in-law, E. Washington Rhodes, a lawyer, succeeded him as editor. While Perry had opposed separate schools and educational discrimination, Rhodes took a much more aggressive position and encouraged blacks to "open fire on segregated schools. Fight against them incessantly and continuously." The new editor instructed parents: "Refuse to permit your child to attend any school other than the one in his district."[19] In the following years, the *Tribune* contributed vital encouragement to the battle against Jim Crow schools in Philadelphia.

Evidence of segregation at both the state and local level included the movement to establish a state normal school for Negroes. In the 1850s, the Quakers established in Philadelphia the Institute for Colored Youth, which in 1904 relocated in Cheyney, a few miles outside of Philadelphia, and concentrated on training Negro teachers. In 1914, the school began to receive minimal state aid, and in 1920, Cheyney became a state normal school. While the public knew that Pennsylvania assumed financial responsibility with the goal of making the institution a colored normal school, it was not officially designated as such until 1923. This occurred despite opposition from many Philadelphia Negroes, who argued that there was a conspiracy in the city among white groups to segregate all colored teacher training in the state by requiring Negroes to attend Cheyney, which had inferior facilities. Graduates of Cheyney, alleged the critics, would then be sent out to teach in the expanding segregated systems of the state. Dissension also troubled the Negro community because some blacks charged the head of Cheyney, Leslie Hill, and teachers there with being partly responsible for the state action. This event appears to have made blacks in Philadelphia even more aware of the segregation trend in the state.[20]

Negroes feared that segregation at the local level was expanding through the use of intelligence quotients to group students in the high schools. Negro girls who entered Girls' High School reported in 1924 that two groups within their grade were composed almost entirely of black students. Only a few Negroes were scattered throughout the rest of the classes. Some of the parents investigated the situation and found that the only white children in these two predominantly Negro groups were special or backward students. A delegation met with the principal and was informed that the groupings were based solely on the results of intelligence tests. The principal protested that there was no way of ascertaining whether a student was white or Negro when the groupings were made. This assertion was quickly repudiated when a black citizen found that an X was placed on the registration cards of Negro students.[21]

The practice of segregation through alleged I.Q. scores was investigated by the NAACP. The group contended that the administrators' claim that all Negroes were together because of low I.Q.s was false. An eighth grade teacher cited the case of a former student with an exceptionally high I.Q. who, nevertheless, was placed in one of the backward groups. The high school reclassified her only after strenuous protest.[22]

Segregation and discrimination in the Girls High School were reported both in the schoolroom and in extracurricular activities. In 1924, an assistant principal informed Negro girls planning to go on the traditional senior trip to Washington that they must make their own reservations in the national capital since they would not be staying with the white students. According to the *Tribune,* this was another example of the efforts made to discourage the Negro girls from going and further evidence of the prejudice "which abounds in the Girls' High School."[23]

Incidents such as these led some black Philadelphians to question whether segregated schools were not defensible because children in black schools did not encounter such disheartening and humiliating experiences. A fourteen-year-old black student in Philadelphia Girls' High School wrote the NAACP in New York in 1923 to express her support for more separate schools. She argued that separate schools staffed by Negro teachers would offer "regeneration" and more incentive for black students.[24]

The precise extent of racial segregation in the schools in the mid-1920s is difficult to determine. Statistics released in 1925 indicate that only 32 of the 201 elementary schools had no black children, although the percentage of Negroes in many of the mixed schools was either very small or extremely high.[25] The same survey did indicate that the number of children in officially designated separate schools had declined. In 1923, 8,718 black children attended these schools, while by 1925 the number had declined to 7,755.[26] However, when a separate black school opened its doors in the fall of 1925, Philadelphia Negroes believed educational policy was directed toward increased segregation, and a new militancy appeared in the black community. Over three hundred students in South Philadelphia were transferred from mixed schools in their immediate neighborhoods to the new separate school. A committee of parents formed after principals at the children's former schools refused to register the pupils. Explanations for the refusals ranged from the candid statement by one principal that the policy was segregation to the hazy generality by another that the schools were crowded.[27]

One hundred and fifty parents, some accompanied by their children, met to organize a protest committee. Robert Bagnall of the New York office of the NAACP, who had led fights against segregation in the schools in Detroit, Dayton, and Canton, attended the meeting and urged that the case be taken to court.[28] When the parents' group met with a member of the superintendent's office, he justified the action on the grounds that congestion in the buildings precipitated the move. He also stated that he was under the impression that Negroes wanted their own schools. He promised to have the plan reevaluated, but the board upheld the policy of mass transfer of Negro students.

Black opposition continued, led by parents whose children had attended Landreth, many blocks away from the new school. Parents boycotted the black school and appeared daily at Landreth demanding that their children be admitted. While parents maintained the boycott, NAACP officials considered launching a court battle over the policy.[29] A. Phillip Randolph, editor of the *Messenger,* applauded the new militant stand of the Philadelphians, but lamented the fact that "our own colored teachers are not right on the issue of segregation in the schools. They hedge and equivocate, bow and kowtow to the hateful spirit of the Bourbon South."[30] He urged the Negro teachers to refuse to teach in a separate school and to send an ultimatum to the board of education stating they would teach only in a mixed school.[31] This recommendation was too radical, for the teachers were fearful of jeopardizing their positions. The boycott, however, was successful because several weeks later some of the Negro children were allowed to register at the mixed schools. The black community exulted over the reversal of the policy but asserted that through the NAACP they would pursue their battle against discrimination and segregation in the schools.[32]

A few months later, the board of education announced that the Singerly School would be designated a colored school and appointed Arthur

Huff Faucett, a member of a respected family in the black community, as principal. The *Tribune* chose this occasion to discuss the connection between segregated schools and other areas of discrimination. The editorial suggested that "by accepting segregated schools we admit that we do not deserve the same kind of treatment accorded other citizens." The result, the paper stated, included "denial of any semblance of representation in the city government, lack of promotion of Negro policemen and firemen, and denial of good positions to black politicians." The antisegregation voice grieved, "Is not the relation between the white and colored people becoming strained in Philadelphia in exact ratio to the number of segregated schools?" The *Tribune* argued that "little skirmishes will do no good." Instead, black citizens must be prepared to face a long battle and many court cases in order to end school segregation in the city.[33]

The Philadelphia branch of the NAACP strenuously objected to the board about the Singerly School. They recalled that two years before they had written proposing an experiment in which colored and white teachers would work together in that school, and if the arrangement went smoothly, the plan could be extended to other schools. Thus, the prohibition on blacks teaching in mixed schools would be phased out. Aside from acknowledging the letter, the board took no further action. The NAACP pleaded for more response. "Self-respecting Negroes of Philadelphia do not feel like they are receiving a square deal from the Board of Education." The NAACP mourned that "nearly 200,000 citizens have no voice in the management of anything connected with the schools which their children attend."

Finally, the NAACP letter foreshadowed the Coleman Report by arguing that any difference in the level of intelligence or scholastic ability of white and Negro children did not justify segregation. "If other children are better and brighter than colored children, then the children of color should by all means come in contact with them daily so as to get the benefit of this superiority." Or, concluded the NAACP, "if the colored children are better and brighter, then they want to be with others in order to help them."[34]

By April, the NAACP was holding meetings throughout the city concerning educational segregation. The Republican party now came under attack because, as one speaker emphasized, the board of education was elected by the board of judges, which was chosen by the Republican organization. Since blacks were solidly Republican, the question arose as to whether the Grand Old Party was betraying the best interests of the Negro. The question was well taken because at no time in the 1920s were most black or white politicians involved in the push for integration of the school facilities. Henry Carter Patterson, chairman of the Philadelphia Inter-racial Committee, instructed citizens that they should no longer rely on appeals for justice to move the board because his committee's investigations "had forced him to conclude that the Board of Public Education as well as the Superintendents are of the opinion that segregation is the best solution to the problem."[35]

The *Tribune,* actively supporting the NAACP efforts to arouse the public, concurred with Patterson that petitions to the board of education were useless. "The Board has been beseeched, begged and threatened, but it remains steadfast to its policy of discrimination," snapped the paper. "We must, therefore, use different methods of attack." The newspaper concluded by urging the initiation of a court case against the board.[36]

The Philadelphia segregation issue became so acute that Dr. Edwin C. Broome, superintendent of schools, agreed to address the annual meeting of the Association of Teachers of Colored Children of Philadelphia. If he intended to alleviate the tension in the black community, he failed, for the following week *Tribune* headlines blazed: "Broome, Philadelphia Superintendent, Feels Negroes are Happier in Own Schools." The superintendent's address, as the newspaper reported, contained some ambiguous statements. The mere fact that Philadelphia Negroes were opposed to a separate school system was no basis upon which the board determined policy, said Broome. "The question of education is general—neither white or colored. No one wants segregated schools but this in itself is no basis upon which we decide as to the advisability of the separate schools." Having implied that Negro groups demanding integration would not influence board decisions, he went on to encourage black factions who desired separate schools. "If colored are more happy together, trained by their own teachers, and ask for a hearing on an educational basis, they will be listened to."[37]

A clearcut example of Philadelphia's segregation policy occurred when schools opened in the fall of 1926. This incident precipitated the first resort to legal action by Negroes against the administration. Roscoe Douglas, a resident of a middle-class, predominantly white area of Germantown and cashier for the Keystone Cooperative Banking Association, presented his six-year-old son for admission at the all-white Keyser School located two blocks from his home. The principal directed the father to register him at a Negro school four blocks from the Douglas residence. Douglas demurred, declaring, "I am not going to send my child four blocks away when this is the school he should attend." He claimed that he had no objection to his child attending a colored school. "I believe colored teachers are just as efficient as are the white, but I don't want my child walking across extra streets to get to school when this is the legal and logical school for him to attend."[38] When he returned to see the principal the next day, she informed him that she had discussed the matter with the superintendent. If the father did not send his son to the Negro school, the child's registration would be canceled since the schools were not compelled to accept a student until he was eight years old. Douglas refused, and the school canceled the child's registration.

A school administrator then told the father that it would be inadvisable to admit the boy at the Keyser School because the school had never had any Negro students and friction might result. The official offered to see that Douglas's son was admitted to a mixed school which was ten blocks away. The father rejected this proposal. Finally, Douglas was informed that the central office had decided "not [to] permit a condition to arise that would overcrowd the Keyser School." School officials assured the father that color had nothing to do with the decision. Douglas replied that the colored school at which he originally was instructed to register his son was so crowded that some classes had to be held in the halls, whereas the white school had no such congestion. When the central office refused to consider the matter further, Douglas filed a writ of mandamus requiring the board of education to show cause why his son should not be admitted to the Keyser School.[39]

The *Tribune* and the local NAACP, recognizing that this could be the test case they needed to bring the board's discrimination policy before the courts, immediately organized support for Douglas. They established the *Philadelphia Tribune* Defense Fund, and Negroes anxious to support the legal battle assembled at a local theatre to demonstrate their objections to current educational policy. Here, local black leaders argued that they must fight school segregation not only because of its educational discrimination, but also because of its social ramifications. Forrester B. Washington, head of the Armstrong Association and later appointed by the state to direct a study of the Negro in Pennsylvania, presided. In his address, Washington underscored the connection between segregation in schools and on the job. "It is generally assumed by the working classes that if it is disgraceful to go to school with a colored person, it is disgraceful to work with them."[40]

The meeting brought out the sharp animosity of these integrationists toward blacks who supported segregation. Samuel Hart, black representative to the state legislature, thundered against two Baptist ministers of South Philadelphia's ghetto, the Reverend William A. Harrod, pastor of the First African Baptist Church, and W. F. Graham, pastor of Holy Trinity Baptist Church, for telling members of the state legislature that segregation was the better plan for Negroes. Philadelphia Baptist ministers, in contrast with most of their Methodist and Presbyterian counterparts, appear to have been advocates of separate schools throughout the period.

The Cheyney College came under attack for allegedly preparing black teachers to enter only Negro schools. The Republican organization also came under fire. "Do not vote the Republican ticket," one speaker urged, "if you feel a candidate on the Democratic ticket has the interests of the race at heart more than candidates running on the Republican ticket."[41] The interest resulting from this call to action made it appear as though the Negro community had finally developed the determination and unity to persevere in their fight against the school system.

The board of education requested and received a continuation of the case in order to prepare its answer. The defense was ingenious. The school administration denied that there was an established rule that the board of education assign pupils to the school nearest their residence. The reply to the writ also argued that the board decided which school a child must attend "for the best interests of the prospective pupil." Finally, the writ claimed that the principal of the white school did not technically refuse to register Robert Douglas in her school because Meehan, the Negro school, was a branch of Keyser. The principal, argued the board, was empowered to use her discretion in determining which branch of the school a child should attend.[42]

The court denied the writ and concurred with the board that a child did not have to be admitted to the school closest to his home.[43] Therefore, the Douglas case did not become the landmark incident which integrationists desired. Nor did the public attention force the board to alter its support of segregation. Three years later, black parents were still trying to force Keyser to admit Negro pupils.[44]

As W.E.B. DuBois claimed when he visited Philadelphia shortly after the incident, "Philadelphia is the best place to discuss race relations because there is more race prejudice here than in any other city in the United States." DuBois railed against not only the traditional apathy of black Philadelphians, but also the poor support Negroes received from white politicians. Noting the recent fight against segregated schools and the protest meetings held, the editor of the *Crisis* condemned "the politicians who could do so much to remedy these evil conditions" because they failed to attend the meeting, "offering flimsy excuses for their absence or sending representatives who cannot represent."[45]

Although the *Tribune* Defense Fund rose to over $1,000 in the next eighteen months, the NAACP did not bring another suit against the board. By 1929, the newspaper struck out against the local NAACP's inactivity in an editorial entitled "The NAACP Needed," which cited the increasing segregation in the city and proclaimed the "need for new blood, clearer vision and a will to fight" by the local NAACP.[46]

Isadore Martin, president of the Philadelphia chapter, responded to the charge in a letter to Walter White, assistant secretary of the national organization. Martin's letter revealed personal friction as well as disagreement over tactics among the antisegregation forces of the city. He complained to White that the *Tribune* editor was " 'sore' because the local officials would not cater to his selfish plans in connection with a small fund raised here to fight segregation in the schools." Martin charged that the *Tribune* committee was trying to "dictate to us what to do," and he therefore thought it inadvisable to accept the fund. He concluded his response to the editorial with the observation, "if after more than two years a paper like the *Tribune* can raise only $1,000 to fight public school segregation, you can easily see how much the people of this city want to do away with segregation."[47]

Martin's defense is more revealing of the type of enervating personal clashes which could impair effective leadership in a sustained push against racial discrimination than it is descriptive of the black Philadelphian's stance on segregated schools. In a community plagued by low income and marked by many pleas for funds by the race's social agencies, charities, and civic groups, a $1,000 fund coupled with all of the public participation in protest meetings suggests a significant degree of concern about Jim Crow schools.

The *Tribune* continued to try to rouse citizens to protest against the school policies, but no positive results were effected in the 1920s. Some-

times the board of education, acknowledging that segregation existed, explained that it occurred "because the colored people had wanted it."
To this statement, the *Tribune* replied, "It is not customary for public officials to grant the desires of colored citizens."[48] On other occasions, the school board denied there was segregation or discrimination. One example of the contradictory stand occurred when a judge of the children's division of the municipal court criticized the board of education in 1929. A thirteen-year-old Negro came before him charged with truancy and stealing. The judge lamented, "I can't send him to the Shallcross or the Elliott House because there is no provision for colored children. The Board of Education is putting up a great number of schools. This is excellent. But there is not one of these schools for colored children."[49]
The Shallcross School, a public school built in the mid-1920s for truant boys, admitted no Negroes. Truant blacks were either treated as criminals and sent to Glen Mills, a school for incorrigibles, or returned to a regular school. Administrators immediately defended themselves. The president of the board, William Raimen, denied any intention on the part of the board of education to discriminate in that institution. "Due to restricted and temporary quarters at the Shallcross School, undoubtedly colored boys have been refused as well as white because the quota was filled." He added, "It is purely a school for truant boys and not for young criminals, and it is not restricted as to color, race or religion."[50]

Two years earlier when a Negro civic worker had unsuccessfully tried to get a black boy admitted to Shallcross, the principal had given a somewhat different explanation. "We do not practice discrimination here," he assured, "and though I can't speak officially, I am sure the Board of Education does not. Of course, in view of the fact that the school is in the experimental stage it would not be expedient for us to admit colored boys at this time." There were plans, he observed, to take care of Negroes in the future. A building for colored boys would be erected adjacent to the white school, and it would be headed by a Negro matron.[51]

Negroes began to devise a strategy to reverse the blatant discrimination. They made two proposals, neither of which was new. One was to get a black appointed to the board so that blacks would have someone in a policy-making position. As early as 1927, the consensus was that Dr. John P. Turner, a prominent Negro physician, was the most qualified candidate. Not until 1935, however, was Turner appointed to the board. A black may finally have been selected as a result of the shifting black political allegiance and the concern Republican politicians now felt about a group they had always considered "safe." In any case, the choice of Turner proved unfortunate. A conservative upper class professional who, like some others among the Negro elite, identified more with the white upper class than with lower socioeconomic groups of his own race, Turner failed to be a consistent defender of black interests.[52]

The second proposal involved altering the school system's policy of not hiring blacks to teach in mixed schools. This practice limited the Negroes' opportunities to teach at the elementary level to the fourteen Negro schools, and also precluded their teaching at the junior or senior high level where only mixed schools existed. In 1928, only 250 of the city's 7,888 teachers were Negro. This number constituted 3.2 percent of the teaching force.[53] But even on this issue blacks split. Negro teachers were not inclined to push for integration in the elementary schools, but instead to argue for the appointment of blacks at the junior and senior high level. A more militant group demanded integration throughout the system. Floyd Logan organized the Educational Equality League in 1932 and quickly fired off a barrage of demands to the board. One of the main issues was the use of dual lists of teacher candidates for appointments in schools. Logan demanded a nonsegregated list. For the first time, a permanent pressure group existed that would tenaciously push for long-range educational goals—a marked contrast to the ephemeral groups which had banded together to combat a single incident and then dissolved. The end of dual lists was realized in July 1937 when seven black educators received appointments in mixed schools and two white teachers were assigned to Negro schools.[54] The league continued its efforts in the following decade and remained the chief pressure group for educational equality in Philadelphia.

The conditions of the Negro teacher improved somewhat in later years, but the black student continued to experience subtle discrimination and frequent segregation. Not until the 1960s did the Philadelphia school system, forced by the federal government, make significant efforts to erase discriminatory practices which had existed through the century.

Perhaps Philadelphia's experience with public education for Negroes, more than that of any other northern city, points up the myriad conditions which allowed segregation and discrimination to flourish in northern schools after World War I. The factors responsible centered around both the rigidity and prejudice of the white community and the disunity and fragmentation of the black community. The attitude of the board toward Negroes was thinly veiled prejudice, and their actions were tempered only slightly by the knowledge that it would be politically inexpedient to try to achieve total segregation. The organization and appointment system of the board enabled it to be relatively unresponsive to Negro demands. This elitist group was disinclined to meet minority needs which did not coincide with their own views of correct educational policy. Their perspective of education for Negroes was also distorted by fear that the system would be overwhelmed by hordes of illiterate southern Negroes who would lower the quality of the student population. Furthermore, they could justify their segregationist inclinations on the grounds that a significant part of the black community had accepted and even supported it because it provided jobs.

Conditions within the black community worked against the kind of cohesion and militance which might have forced administrators to alter their segregation policies. For the majority of the period, Philadelphia's black leaders relied on petitions and conferences with the board—"the better thinking classes" of the white and black community, as one petition termed them.[55] They placed their faith in relatively low-keyed discussions and in each group's sense of justice. These leaders eschewed direct action except in the 1925 school boycott and resorted in only one instance to legal action to try to block the board's policies. Destructive divisions and power rivalries among leaders, common in both black and white communities, also blunted the effectiveness of the black community.

But the migrants and even the Philadelphia-born low-income blacks contributed to the fragmentation. The day-to-day pressures of making a living were so great, and the tradition of participating in permanent pressure groups so slight, that it was difficult to mold their numbers into an effective group which could persistently work against educational discrimination. Also, black politicians and educators, two important parts of the small but vital middle class which could provide leadership, did not dare risk their coveted and hard-earned positions by participation. All of these factors therefore produced a weak front against the board which the school administrators were not only aware of but relied on throughout the period.

Finally, a critical factor producing education segregation was the growth of the ghetto itself. As more and more blocks became solidly black in South and West Philadelphia as a result of continued black migration and white flight, the neighborhood schools reflected this racial separation and produced more educational experiences for Philadelphia children devoid of significant racial mixing.

INDIANAPOLIS

In 1916, before Indianapolis experienced the full force of southern migration, the *Freeman* answered an inquiry about race relations in the city by commenting that "there is very little race friction, but the possibility is here as it is elsewhere." Reflecting the pragmatic passiveness which Indianapolis blacks had maintained over the years, the newspaper went on to observe that "the colored people carefully avoid it [race friction], knowing what it means to give cause for agitation."[56] Although Negroes were anxious to preserve the fragile community peace, the following ten years were to embroil them in bitter disputes and court battles over increased segregation and discrimination. While in recent years local white residents and schoolmen have blamed the deterioration of race relations in the 1920s on the Ku Klux Klan's grip on the state, the tension began to develop before the rise of the Klan and involved many whites, including school administrators who never embraced the white supremacy organization. Ample evidence suggests that the rapid increase in the black population during and directly after World War I precipitated the racial hostility and brought on the blanket segregation policy of the 1920s, which left such monuments as segregated schools by 1930.

Tension rapidly developed in two areas of race relations, housing and education. Chapter 1 discusses the white reaction to black efforts to move into neighborhoods outside the Negro district. However, it is important to recognize that the battle against residential segregation occupied the time and resources of Negro leaders in Indianapolis and sapped attention and energy which otherwise might have been devoted to the second area of conflict, the schools.

In 1917, one educator who studied Indianapolis schools observed that "the presence of a black child in a white school causes unnecessary attention and sometimes unpleasant comment."[57] The number of black children attending mixed schools was minimal, for in 1916 the *Freeman* estimated that probably no mixed elementary school had more than half a dozen Negro children.[58] Frequently, even the enrollment of a few Negro students produced protests from white parents and petitions to the board for more colored schools. The filing of such petitions was generally followed by petitions from Negro parents objecting to such requests. At the high school level no segregation existed, and Negroes attended all three high schools. Negro high school students nevertheless had to endure insults and some isolation. One student recalled that on enrolling in Shortridge High School he, along with the rest of the Negroes, was instructed to sit in the back of the room. When he made the highest grade on the first test, the student was rewarded with the command, "Sit up here with the white pupils."[59]

As the Negroes streamed into the city, more Negro children appeared in the white schools, but the number was still small. Most of the migrants' children were channeled into the segregated schools, and soon the administration began to discuss the need for more teachers for backward children in the colored schools.[60]

In 1918, 81.4 percent of all black students were enrolled in separate elementary schools; by 1922, over 90 percent of the Negro children were segregated.[61] White parents objected to any mixing and began to push for a separate black high school. Many schoolmen and board members supported such a plan. In 1922, Principal George Buck of Shortridge High School, the most prestigious of the city's high schools, informed the board that he believed a separate high school should be established for Negro students.[62] This proposal was reinforced by a petition submitted by the Indianapolis Chamber of Commerce the same day. The petition stated "that in the development of a complete high school system for the city, proper attention should be given to the necessity for a separate modern completely equipped and adequate high school building for colored students."[63]

The move for a black high school gained numerous supporters in the city and brought forth varied arguments justifying segregation. The Indiana Federation of Community Civic Clubs submitted a resolution which cited statistics showing that, although blacks constituted about 10 percent of the population, 25 percent of the deaths in the city were among Negroes. Pointing out that the public schools had a large number of Negro children with incipient tuberculosis, the group suggested the remedy of erecting a cordon sanitaire through separate schools staffed by Negro teachers.[64]

On December 12, 1922, the Committee on Instruction recommended to the board that a separate high school be established. Citing the large number of Negro high school pupils, the committee extolled their "laud-

able desire" for a high school education. They suggested that the fullest
opportunity for the realization of this desire should be supported by the
administration. They ingeniously explained that "the maximum educational opportunity for these pupils will be provided for by a new modern,
well equipped high school. Such a school," the committee posited, "will
provide the fullest opportunity for the development of initiative and
self-reliance and the other qualities needed for good citizenship." A mo-
tion to create a separate Negro high school followed the report, and all
four commissioners voted in favor of the proposal.[65]

The decision did not come without protest from outraged blacks. The
prospect of a separate high school mobilized the black community, and
petitions against the proposal swamped the board. Negroes argued against
a black high school on a variety of grounds, including the additional expense and its un-American as well as un-Christian implications.[66] Afro-
American high school pupils, despite the discrimination they encountered
in mixed schools, were "almost one hundred per cent" against the plan.[67]

The decision to segregate students at the high school level did not blunt
the demands to get Negro students out of the elementary schools. Thus,
in 1923 the board drew new boundaries for fourteen Negro elementary
schools and required Negroes living in all of these areas to attend the
separate schools.[68] The changes in boundaries removed children from
predominantly white schools and caused them to travel much further to
attend the separate schools. Jonathan Artist petitioned the board to allow
his children to remain in the mixed school they were attending because it
was much closer than the one to which they were transferred. Artist
resented the two-mile walk to the new school, which involved crossing
many railroad tracks. Not only did the commissioners reject Artist's
plea, but they also refused his request to grant his children carfare so
that they might make the trip by streetcar.[69]

Two black parents turned to the courts for support of their contention
that legally the children should be allowed to attend the school closest to
their homes. The court, however, declared that the board of education
had the authority to transfer the children to whatever school it deemed
appropriate. The massive transfers involved in this new redistricting meant
that elementary schools were almost totally white or completely Negro.[70]

The administration had originally stressed the superior modern building
and equipment which Negro high school students would have. In 1924, as
the plans were initiated for construction, one commissioner suggested that

in the interest of economy, instead of erecting a new building for the black high school, the old Shortridge High School be converted to the Negro school since plans were under way for a new white high school.[71] The board rejected this proposal and proceeded with plans to construct a new building for the Negro students. Blacks were not mollified by the prospect of a modern structure and became even more hostile to the proposed high school when the board announced that it had selected a site. Blacks declared the location, which was two blocks from a glue factory that emitted noxious fumes, totally unsatisfactory. The area was also near a dumping ground and municipal sewage disposal station. The *Freeman* suggested that the location was selected because of its obscurity. The paper scornfully described the board as "the Lily White Crew" who were "ashamed of the crime of segregation they are perpetrating upon the community" and were "trying to hide their blunder in an unpaved side street."[72]

While the commissioners were making plans for the new black high school, they were also locating funds for a new building for Shortridge High School. White parents, many of them civic leaders, urged that Shortridge be relocated on the Indianapolis north side, an area far removed from any black neighborhoods. It was evident that the location was proposed because it would eliminate Negro students. One of the prominent women's clubs issued a report on Shortridge which pointed out that the school should be relocated because of the "numbers of colored students packed into crowded classrooms with the white children."[73]

Whatever hopes administrators had that a $500,000 building staffed by Negroes would lessen the black community's hostility were dashed when a number of Negroes in conjunction with the NAACP filed a suit to block construction of the school. Archie Greathouse, a Negro restaurant owner and chief plaintiff, claimed that the school would not be equal since it could not provide the specialized training offered by the technical high schools as well as a college preparatory course similar to that at Shortridge. He also asserted in the complaint that facilities would be unequal because more money was spent for other schools.[74]

When a local court ruled in favor of the school board, the black group appealed the decision. In 1926, the supreme court of Indiana heard the case. But the last hope of Indianapolis Negroes vanished when the court handed down a decision sustaining the lower court's decision. The supreme court would not issue an injunction against construction of the school. The decision stated that the mere apprehension and fears that the school would be unequal were not sufficient grounds for an injunction.[75]

The NAACP's annual report declared that the Greathouse decision was a striking example of the attempt to institute segregated schools in northern communities. The group feared that "if the segregationists are successful in that city, the movement will spread to other parts of the state, and will . . . start similar practices in other border and northern states."[76]

In 1926, only 90 Negroes out of 2,931 students were enrolled at Shortridge; 249 out of 3,532 pupils at Manual Tech; and 189 out of 5,697 students at Arsenal Tech.[77] Nevertheless, all of these students who would still be in high school the following fall would have to attend the Negro school, which had been named Crispus Attucks. The policy was thus established which remained in effect for the next twenty years: Indianapolis would have no mixing whatsoever of Negro and white high school students.

In 1927, Crispus Attucks opened with 1,300 Negro students. The black community responded to the school in several ways. One group, irrevocably opposed to segregation, gave the school no support. Another group, especially some black teachers, were more than accepting of the new institution, which provided over forty new jobs and which also might build racial solidarity. This group had remained officially silent during the debate about the building of Attucks because of prevailing opposition to it among most of the city's blacks. J. Morton-Finney, a Negro teacher in Indianapolis who later became principal of Attucks, wrote a revealing article for *School and Society* in 1926 which suggests some of the views this group held. Morton-Finney considered the arguments for and against segregated schools, and concluded that because "Englishmen are best qualified by nature and natural law and right of self-determination to educate Englishmen . . . and so on through the several groups of races and nationalities . . . Negroes should teach Negroes."[78] Morton-Finney argued that segregation should therefore be viewed "as a form of functional specialization in division of labor rather than a form of proscription for the satisfaction of racial greed, lust, exploitation and diabolical selfishness."[79] He rejected the idea that contact in the classroom between whites and Negroes was that beneficial and termed as "theory rather than fact" any extracurricular mingling of the two races in integrated schools. Morton-Finney saw educational segregation as "the anvil on which can be hammered into being a powerful Negro nation."[80]

The influence which Morton-Finney and those of similar attitudes had

on events was probably minimal because the board's actions were determined by the members' own prejudices and by pressure from the white
community. The tacit support for segregation, however, of an important
segment of the small Negro middle class meant the loss of potential leaders
in the Negro community's fight against segregated schools.

Another group of black citizens viewed the establishment of a separate
school as unjust but determined to see the modern facilities utilized to
provide quality education so that black high school students would not
suffer academically. One Negro reflected this sentiment of many Indianapolis blacks in a series of articles for the *Indianapolis Recorder* on "the
meaning of a colored high school." Reflecting on the motives which
prompted the building of the new school, he wrote: "We know the kind
of heart that gave it. . . . It is the heart revealed in the Nordic ravings of
Lanthrop [*sic*] Stoddard. It is the heart of the Ku Klux Klan." He declared, "If we were independent; if we were strong, with voices in unison
we would have fared differently." But given the present condition, the
author urged the black community to make the high school one of excel-
lence by giving it full community support.[81]

The school did have some impressive facilities. Attucks received the
first organ in Indiana schools, for example. But the board made it obvious
that no social interaction between white and Negro students was acceptable.
Black high school pupils were not allowed to use white school auditoriums
or to compete with white students in athletics. Thus, the Attucks football
teams had to travel all over the state as well as to Illinois, Missouri, and
Kentucky for contests with black schools. In Indianapolis, only the Catholic
High School, which had been integrated from the time it opened in the
1920s, would play Attucks teams.[82]

The members of the Indianapolis Board of School Commissioners
elected in 1925 were supported by the Ku Klux Klan. As Emma Lou
Thornbrough has shown, however, this school board did not initiate any
new segregation policies but merely enforced and carried to completion
the policies which an earlier school board had initiated.[83] The school board
which ordered the erection of Attucks was composed of respected civic
leaders who had no Klan affiliations and were supported by the Citizens
School Community which worked against the Klan-affiliated slate elected
in 1925.[84] Hence, the responsibility for policies which locked segregation
into the system lay not with the Klan but with civic leaders and school
administrators who held views on racial issues similar to those of the
Invisible Empire.

The board was so anxious to avoid any mixing of white and black students that in 1927 it financed a limited program of reverse busing of Negro children. The policy arose when a two-room portable Negro school, Number 65, was declared unfit and the children ordered to attend a distant segregated school. One father of three pupils at Number 65 requested that the children be allowed to attend school Number 73, a white school, which was only one-half mile from his home. His salary was only thirteen dollars per week, and he could not afford to pay the carfare for his children to attend the black school. The board moved that all the students who had attended the portable unit would have to transfer to the colored school, but that the school system would pay for the children's transportation.[85] Black citizens protested, and some of the students involved became truant in retaliation. The board delayed the move until summer, but then enforced the transfers.

Despite the 1923 redistricting of black elementary schools, a few schools still had some Negroes enrolled. In 1929, the commissioners moved to end this minuscule integration by transferring all Negro children from three mixed schools to segregated schools. A delegation of Negroes pleaded with the board of school commissioners to reconsider the transfers from one school in particular. They stated that because of the long distance to the newly assigned schools, eighteen children, from six to eight years of age, would have to go by streetcar and cross busy intersections. They decried this "suicide step."

The superintendent rejected their arguments and justified the transfer on the basis that it would ease discipline problems. He explained that in order "to reduce the friction, which naturally has crept out in the school, we tried to solve the problem by transferring these colored children to other schools." The discipline problem of Negro children, he said, "is a problem that comes up in all these situations and for the good of all concerned, we have thought the conditions warranted the transfer."[86] The board upheld the transfers. This reassignment of students was the final step in establishing the largest segregated system in any northern metropolitan area.

The Negro community could now do little to pry open the segregated system. In 1929, the NAACP campaigned against the board members who were running in the municipal election, basing their campaign not on segregated schools but on a plea for equal salaries for white and black teachers. Yet, even this demand went unheeded. In the 1930s, the salaries of Negro teachers continued to average from $300 to $1,000 per year less than those of white teachers. This contrast in earnings was significant since many Negro teachers earned under $1,200 per year.[87]

By 1930, Indianapolis schools symbolized the successful efforts of northern racists to erect two separate school systems which were almost as rigid as similar dual systems in the South. It remained an impregnable rampart in the city's efforts to segregate the two races until 1949, when the first integration policy within the schools was grudgingly introduced.

The increasing segregation in Indianapolis schools throughout the early twentieth century delineates clearly the pattern which to a lesser extent existed in many northern cities. Minimal mixing of the races had been tolerated as long as it involved relatively few Negro students. After World War I, however, the growing number of black children in the schools hardened the white community's opposition to integration and mobilized support for comprehensive segregation.

It did not take the Klan to implement further segregation: civic leaders and educators were the spearheads. In the face of such determination by whites, the black community, despite its numbers, was relatively powerless. Turning to the only means that might have blocked further segregation, the courts, they found no support, but rather reinforcement of the racist policies. Indianapolis Negroes, traditionally conservative, had neither the power nor the disposition to fight the action further. For them, living in a northern rather than a southern city brought better schools so far as facilities, but no better situation in the area of racial mixing in the schools.

CHICAGO

Even before the Great Migration, American Negroes conceived of Chicago as a black mecca, rivaled only by New York's Harlem. The *Indianapolis Freeman* heralded Chicago as "heaven," observing that some Negroes went "so far as to insist that when a colored person dies in Indianapolis, . . . they will be seen afterwards in that city."[88] Influenced by the *Defender*'s glowing accounts of freedom in the midwestern metropolis, southern Negroes, according to William Tuttle, Jr., viewed Chicago not only as a city but as "a state of mind."[89]

But Chicago fell far short of being a black mecca. *The Negro in Chicago*, the report of the Chicago Commission on Race Relations, publicly documented the city's racism. The blue ribbon commission, appointed following the 1919 race riot, made a searching study not only of factors which immediately precipitated the riot but also of the long-term racial conditions which existed in the city. A portion of the study dealt with education, a facet of the social system which functioned in subtle yet insidious ways against the equal integrated education that the school system officially supported.

The commission found it difficult to evaluate the racial policies of the Chicago school system. According to the administrators, there was no discrimination, all children were treated alike, and no records were kept designating children as either Negro or white. Therefore, they could not provide figures of Negro enrollment or a list of schools which were predominantly black. Scrutiny of the policy of the board of education as revealed in the minutes of the meetings of that group was similarly unenlightening. The schoolmen often implemented policies such as redistricting or massive transfers which blacks contended were directed against mixing of the races, but official records did not reflect such motives. Thus, it was, and remains, difficult to identify many of the policies which discriminated against black students.

Through their own research, the commission ascertained that ten elementary schools were at least 70 percent Negro and twelve more were between 13 and 70 percent black.[90] Racial segregation in the schools existed primarily because of racial segregation in residential areas. White opposition to black encroachments beyond the increasingly congested Black Belt was so effective that residential segregation increased by 13 percent between 1910 and 1920 and another 13 percent by 1930.[91] Therefore, by 1930, when twenty-six schools were 85 to 100 percent black, the main cause was the commitment of white Chicagoans to restrict all blacks to the South Side black metropolis.[92] As one historian has observed, white voices demanding a racially segregated school system from 1910 to 1920 fell mute in the 1920s because the growing residential segregation accomplished the same purpose.[93]

The ghetto alone, however, did not account for all of the racial isolation in Chicago schools. Other causes of segregation of the races resulted from the conscious efforts of educators. The segregation policies of individual schools were frequently the result of the principal's prejudice. Possibly the most blatant case of the effect of a principal's racial attitudes occurred at the Fuller School, which was a branch of Felsenthal and was headed by the same principal. Felsenthal was located in a neighborhood where 38 percent of the residents were Negro, and 42 percent of the people living in Fuller's district were black. Yet, Fuller had a Negro student body of 90 percent while Felsenthal had only 20 percent Negroes. According to investigators for the Commission on Race Relations, the principal believed in separate schools and therefore tried to place as many of her Negro students as possible in Fuller which was rundown, neglected, and had no playground.[94]

Other schools showed similarly disproportionate high and low percentages of Negroes when compared with the racial composition of neighborhoods. In the Mosely School, for instance, 70 percent of the students were black, while the Negroes constituted only 46 percent of the neighborhood.[95] Such figures gave credence to Negroes' contentions that through redistricting, transfers, and other discriminatory devices, some school officials were determined to maintain certain schools as primarily white or black.

Within mixed schools, cases of segregation and discrimination existed. Wendell Phillips High School, which Negroes frequently complained about, affords an example. The school was rapidly becoming a predominantly Negro school during World War I, and by 1920, blacks constituted 56 percent of the student body. Proposed segregation of a student cadet company by the white officer in charge during the war was rejected by the principal. Much to the relief of Negroes, the principal declared that Negroes were in the band and on the school teams; therefore, if the officer wanted to segregate the company, he would have to get permission from the board of education.[96] Frequently, the position of the school was less supportive of integrated programs. In 1918, incidents of segregation in the high school's night classes enraged the *Defender* and precipitated protests. Negro students alleged that room assignments produced all-white and all-black rooms. One teacher justified the action by claiming that "whites mastered their studies easier than the colored pupils." When a black student enrolled and asked to be assigned to a room with white students, she was refused and told to report to another room where students of her race were being instructed.[97]

Wendell Phillips also had no mixed social activities. By 1920, no school social affairs occurred that were not by invitation. No Negroes were invited to these events, which were held by school clubs that excluded black students. The principal refused to prohibit this policy "until he saw the parents of the children mixing socially."[98]

Englewood and Hyde Park high schools had much smaller percentages of black students than Wendell Phillips, and the principals of these schools reported numerous transfer requests from Phillips. In the case of Negro students allowed to transfer out of Phillips, frequently the transfers were later arbitrarily revoked and the students had to return to Phillips.[99]

Phillips became increasingly segregated not only because of the board's willingness to grant transfers out of Phillips to white students, but also because in 1926 school officials removed six of the ten predominantly white elementary schools from the Phillips district. Superintendent William McAndrew described the shift as desirable because of the futility of convincing white students to attend Phillips.[100]

The greatest degree of racial friction occurred at the high school level, and on occasion, student prejudice made it impossible for Negro students to remain in primarily white high schools. One case involved thirty Negroes who enrolled at Tilden but were so harassed by white students that they had to withdraw. Two white pupils at Tilden described their actions as follows: "We didn't give them any peace in the locker room, basement, at noon hours or between classes—told them to keep out of our way—they know where they belong."[101]

While individual cases of prejudice by principals, teachers, or students were familiar and irksome to Negroes, a far more ominous threat appeared in 1918 when a member of the board of education, Max Loeb, began to investigate the feasibility of establishing segregated schools on a citywide basis. Loeb sent a letter to fifty Negro leaders which posed the question: "How best can the Race antagonisms be avoided which so often spring up when the two races are brought into close juxtaposition—especially when white and colored children are in attendance under the same teachers and in the same classes?"

Loeb's letter asked for the men's opinions on several alternatives: separate schools for whites and blacks, or separate classes for the two races, with Negro and white teachers in the same school. Loeb gingerly presented these questions and stressed that "it seems much wiser to have separation (if any at all is necessary) by voluntary action rather than through the operation of the law."[102]

Loeb suggested several alternatives as to how separation might be effected: conferences between white and black leaders; recommendation of the local boards of education; or withdrawal of Negro children upon recommendation of their own leaders from primarily white schools, and registration in schools where Negroes predominated. Loeb's conciliatory closing in his letter which referred to whites and Negroes fighting side by side on the battlefield did little to veil the message Negroes found repugnant. The *Defender* vigorously attacked Loeb's proposals and advised Negro leaders who received the letter to ignore it.[103] Blacks feared that the entire board of education was contemplating segregation and that the letter was the precursor of more segregation. Mayor William Thompson denounced the letter and assured a Negro delegation that "there is no more danger of segregation in the city of Chicago than [of] the Kaiser to be President of the United States."[104] The violent opposition of the Negro leaders caused Loeb to drop the issue, and it was not apparent to what extent other board members had supported these views.

The board members' views on the issue of segregation were somewhat ambivalent when the issue arose on other occasions, but many white Chicagoans wanted no mixing of the races. In 1917, a delegation of white parents, living in the Wendell Phillips District, came before the board requesting that the school body locate a new junior high school at the Willard School, which was not in the Black Belt. They justified the request by citing the number of saloons and poolrooms around the Phillips School. When pressed, they divulged their real motivation, which was to keep their children from attending classes with Negroes. One of the board members, Edward J. Piggatt, demanded, "Don't you know that there is no Jim Crow law in this state?" Loeb, however, took a different position and recommended that the board "take the Negro leaders into a conference, and perhaps we may work out some solution."[105]

While separate schools were not officially sanctioned, some all-black or all-white schools resulted from carefully drawn South Side elementary school boundary lines. Michael Homel's study of boundaries which were drawn in 1921 and remained in effect for the next twenty years reveals that "school officials honored at almost every point the black belt's eastern boundary, Cottage Grove Ave." Yet, Homel discovered that the western boundary, Wentworth Avenue, was not consistently followed in establishing the elementary school boundary line. He concluded that the political influence and prosperity of the white Cottage Grove residents (which in the 1930s included the mayor and the school board president) influenced the school board "to help hold the line" against racial mixing on the eastern edge. Unlike the organized, politically savvy Cottage Grove group, the white community west of the Black Belt was predominantly lower and lower middle class, lacking organization and political influence. Hence, the board was not effectively pressured by this group to preserve racial separation in those neighborhood schools.[106]

The most flagrant example of the way administrators used boundary lines to achieve de facto segregated schools occurred in the Morgan Park District, an area notorious for its racial prejudice. When a new elementary school, Shoop, was opened in the fall of 1926, the area surrounding it was redistricted in such a way that all Negro pupils residing in the district were transferred to Shoop while all white elementary students would attend Esmond. Negro students frequently had to walk past Esmond in order to get to Shoop, and when their parents tried to register them at Esmond, they were turned away. In one instance, a white child living with a Negro family was permitted to attend Esmond, while the Negro children in the home had to go to Shoop.

Responsibility for establishing this policy lay with the district superintendent. A committee of five black citizens, armed with a petition protesting the situation signed by 130 Negroes, confronted the board of education in November. William Hedges, the district superintendent, was also present. He responded by claiming that he had been following instructions and that no discrimination existed in the district. The acting chairman of the board promised that there would be no discrimination, while implying that Schoop was new and well-equipped and that Negroes should be content with the arrangement.[107]

The board did not subsequently alter the policy, so in January irate Negroes scheduled a protest meeting. Mt. Hope Baptist Church was filled the night of the meeting with outraged Morgan Park residents who demanded an end to the segregation. Representatives of the local branch of the NAACP, the Urban League, and other organizations pledged their support to the movement against the school officials. An attorney was retained as counsel by the citizens, and plans were made to take the case to court if the school committee of the city council refused to act. By May, nothing had been accomplished, and the Chicago branch of the NAACP and the Citizen's Committee of Morgan Park filed mandamus proceedings against the school authorities to show cause why Negro children were not allowed to attend the Esmond School.

In July, the case was heard, and black citizens' hopes for rectification of the situation were dashed by the circuit court decision. The bench sustained the board's demurrer to the writ on the grounds that the Negro citizen's attorney had no records of the board in his bill showing that segregation had been ordered in the schools of the Morgan Park District. Both the attorney and the Negro community were dismayed over the decision because they knew it would be impossible to locate any records of the board which would show official sanction of segregated schools.[108] The Negroes' first response was to amend the writ and take the case to court again. However, they were not able to sustain community interest and financial support, and no further action resulted.

White opposition to even minimal racial mixing dramatically surfaced again in 1928 at Fenger High School when twenty-five Negro girls transferred into the school in order to take household arts courses which were unavailable at Morgan Park High School. This increase in the black enrollment from twenty to forty-five in a school of two thousand students triggered a four-day boycott by white students. Although Fenger's principal and Superintendent William Bogan condemned the student boycott and pledged their support to the black students, their position shifted after the boycott ended. The superintendent then instructed the black students to return to Morgan and promised that household arts would be added to the Morgan Park curriculum.[109]

Relations between the black community and school administrators remained strained, and mutual suspicion marked their interaction. In 1929, Superintendent Bogan conferred with black and white educators and citizens about problems of black children in the schools. Bogan applauded the ability of the two races "to sit down and sanely and with reason discuss problems that confront them in and outside the schools." By the end of the meeting, however, a heated discussion arose and both groups questioned the other's veracity. Black speakers cited cases of discrimination in the schools and lashed out against the transfer system which they believed indicated "an organized effort on the part of someone to bring about separate schools." Bogan admitted that some whites did want segregated schools, but he added that he saw no evidence of such intention by members of the board of education. Responding to accusations about the prejudice of some South Side principals, he acknowledged that some of them might be prejudiced. "They have their prejudice the same as others." But he assured the black citizens that "I resent injustice and would be the last one to defend a school principal who practiced it." Bogan then leveled his criticism at some of the complaints by the Negroes. He stated that he had in his pocket at that time an anonymous letter filled with false complaints about conditions in South Side schools. "They are all lies," he asserted, "nothing but lies."[110]

Whatever unfounded accusations arose on occasion did not alter the fact that by 1930 approximately 27,700 of the 36,962 Negro children enrolled in the Chicago schools attended what one education authority labeled "practically segregated schools."[111] Furthermore, the separate black schools had begun to reflect significant contrasts in school expenditures when compared with appropriations for white schools. Michael Homel has determined that in 1920 the average expenditure for a white pupil was $1.40, or 3 percent higher than that for blacks. By 1930, the discrepancy had jumped to 6 percent, when the expenditure for the white student was $4.35 higher than that for the black child.[112]

Discrimination against black teachers also existed in the Chicago system. Only 2.29 percent of the teaching staff was black, and most of the 304 Negro educators were placed in elementary schools. Only a few blacks taught at the junior and senior high level.[113] Of the 345 principals in the system, only one was black. Her appointment was in "one of the smallest, oldest, and most poorly equipped [schools] in the city."[114]

Conditions did not alter for the better in the following decades. By 1963, one critic of Chicago schools stated that de facto segregation was far less in the 1920s than it was in the 1960s.[115] Transfers and redistricting remained a familiar device to produce the deliberate segregation Negroes had fought from the early decades of the century. At the end of the 1920s, Negroes were in a frustrating position in Chicago. Their city had the reputation of being "the top of the world" for blacks.[116] In fact, it did surpass many other metropolitan areas as far as opportunities for Afro-Americans were concerned. Black Chicagoans were held up as examples by Negroes in other cities because of their activism and political power. Total segregation was no longer a fear by the 1920s—the incident with Loeb had proved the impossibility of implementing such a plan. Yet, the Negroes' position was far from secure. For all their reputed power, they could not even get a Negro appointed to the board of education, a goal they had tried to realize since the early years of the century. Moreover, they were unable to block obvious cases of segregation, such as that which occurred in the Morgan Park schools. Nor could they end the more subtle but effective means of separating the races through transfers and redistricting. Finally, they were helpless to combat the growing number of segregated neighborhood schools that accompanied increased residential segregation. Chicago Negroes therefore had far less power to effect equal integrated education for their children than other black communities realized or than they themselves were willing to admit.

Negroes fought against segregation during the early decades of the century because they realized what the federal government and American society did not begin to acknowledge until the 1950s—that separate but equal schools did not exist, that segregated schools were inherently unequal. Northern cities, however, just as southern hamlets, were not prepared to accept this fact in the early twentieth century. Cities which had been willing to tolerate and even accept the mixing of the races in the schools when relatively few Negroes were involved retreated to a more conscious segregationist position when large numbers of blacks entered the cities desiring homes, jobs, and education.

Because Negroes lacked power, and in many instances unity, their efforts to combat education segregation as well as other forms of discrimination were generally ineffectual or temporary. Not only were they impotent because of their own race's position in American society, but also because courts, city officials, and school administrators were opposed to an educational policy that was free of discrimination. Thus, school leaders introduced various devices during this period which remained in effect for decades and which insured that mixed schools and equal education for all races would remain an ideal rather than a fact.

NOTES

1. August Meier and Elliott Rudwick, *From Plantation to Ghetto,* Rev. ed. (New York: Hill and Wang, 1970), p. 213.

2. Tuttle, *Race Riot,* p. 76.

3. Karl E. and Alma F. Taeuber, *Negroes in Cities: Residential Segregation and Neighborhood Change* (Chicago: Aldine Publishing Co., 1965), pp. 53-55.

4. Interview with Mrs. Marion Minton at her home, Germantown, Pennsylvania, January 29, 1972.

5. Mossell, "Standard of Living," p. 177.

6. *Philadelphia Tribune,* March 23, 1912.

7. Bureau of Compulsory Education, Philadelphia, *Annual Reports,* 1915 and 1918, quoted in Boyer, *Adjustment of a School,* p. 23.

8. *Philadelphia Tribune,* December 11, 1943.

9. Letter, Sadie Mossell to NAACP Headquarters, n.d., Box C-270, Library of Congress, NAACP File.

10. *Philadelphia Tribune,* April 28, 1917.

11. Ibid.

12. Ibid.

13. *Philadelphia Tribune,* December 11, 1920.

14. Committee on Public School Education and Race Relations of the NAACP to Philadelphia Board of Public Education, n.d., in Complete *Minutes,* June 13, 1922.

15. Ibid.

16. Ibid.

17. William Lloyd Imes to Philadelphia Board of Public Education, December 13, 1922, in Complete *Minutes,* December 18, 1922.

18. Lieberson, *Ethnic Patterns in American Cities,* p. 122.

19. *Philadelphia Tribune,* January 30, 1926.

20. "Tragedy of 'Jim Crow,' " *Crisis* 26 (August 1923): 171.

21. *Philadelphia Tribune,* February 9, 1924.

22. *Philadelphia Tribune,* February 16, 1924.

23. *Philadelphia Tribune,* October 10, 1925.

24. Letter, Mary Isabelle Coleman to NAACP Headquarters, July 26, 1923, Box C-288, Library of Congress, NAACP File.

25. Woofter, *Negro Problems in Cities,* p. 178.

26. Ibid.

27. *Philadelphia Tribune,* September 12, 1925.

28. *Philadelphia Tribune,* September 19, 1925.

29. Letter, Julian St. George White to Robert Bagnall, September 30, 1925, Box G-186, Library of Congress, NAACP File.

30. Ibid.

31. Ibid.

32. *Philadelphia Tribune,* October 10, 1925.

33. *Philadelphia Tribune,* January 30, 1926.

34. Letter, Philadelphia Branch of the NAACP to Philadelphia Board of Public Education, February 6, 1926, in Complete *Minutes,* February 26, 1926.

35. *Philadelphia Tribune,* April 3, 1926.

36. *Philadelphia Tribune,* April 10, 1926.

37. *Philadelphia Tribune,* May 22, 1926.

38. *Philadelphia Tribune,* October 23, 1926.

39. Ibid.

40. *Philadelphia Tribune,* December 11, 1926.

41. Ibid.

42. *Philadelphia Tribune,* January 1, 1927.

43. *Philadelphia Tribune,* January 29, 1927.

44. *Philadelphia Tribune,* October 16, 1930.

45. *Philadelphia Tribune,* February 19, 1927.

46. *Philadelphia Tribune,* July 11, 1929.

47. Letter, Isadore Martin to Walter White, July 25, 1928, Box G-187, Library of Congress, NAACP File.

48. *Philadelphia Tribune,* July 18, 1929.

49. Letter, E. Washington Rhodes to Philadelphia Board of Public Education, February 19, 1929, in Complete *Minutes,* March 12, 1929.

50. *Philadelphia Tribune,* February 21, 1929.

51. *Philadelphia Tribune,* May 7, 1927.

52. Nelson, "Race and Class Consciousness," pp. 165-166.

53. *Philadelphia Tribune,* May 10, 1928.

54. Nelson, "Race and Class Consciousness," p. 181.

55. Committee on Public School Education and Race Relations of the NAACP to Philadelphia Board of Public Education, n.d., in Complete *Minutes,* June 13, 1922.

56. *Indianapolis Freeman,* November 18, 1916.

57. Mame Charlotte Mason, "The Policy of Segregation in the Public Schools of Ohio, Indiana, and Illinois" (M.A. thesis, University of Chicago, 1917), p. 25.

58. *Indianapolis Freeman,* November 18, 1916.

59. Ramsey, "Hoosier Negro Teacher," p. 38.

60. Indianapolis Board of School Commissioners, *Minutes,* Book S, April 10, 1917, p. 294.

61. Woofter, *Negro Problems in Cities,* p. 179.

62. Indianapolis Board of School Commissioners, *Minutes,* Book W, September 19, 1922, p. 396.

63. Ibid.

64. Ibid., June 13, 1922, p. 227.

65. Ibid., Box X, December 12, 1922, p. 64.

66. Ibid., November 28, 1922, p. 29.

67. Ramsey, "Hoosier Negro Teacher," p. 30.

68. Indianapolis Board of School Commissioners, *Minutes,* Book Y, September 25, 1923, p. 160.

69. Ibid., September 25, 1923, p. 159.

70. Ibid., January 29, 1924, pp. 304-305.

71. Ibid., February 14, 1924, p. 319.

72. *Indianapolis Freeman,* June 28, 1924.

73. Indianapolis Board of School Commissioners, *Minutes,* Book Y, February 14, 1924, p. 321.

74. *Indianapolis Freeman,* May 24, 1924.

75. *Greathouse v. Board of School Commissioners of City of Indianapolis,* 198 Ind. 95-107 (1926).

76. National Association for the Advancement of Colored People, Seventeenth *Annual Report* (1926), p. 24.

77. Helen Louise Rhodes, "Negro Education in Indiana" (M.A. thesis, Butler University, 1935), p. 32.

78. J. Morton-Finney, "Negro Educators for Negro Education," *School and Society* 24 (November 20, 1926): 626.

79. Ibid., p. 627.

80. Ibid., pp. 627-628.

81. A. H. Maloney, "The Negro of Indianapolis," *Indianapolis Recorder,* April 21, 1928.

82. Robert Allen Lowe, "Racial Segregation in Indiana, 1920-1950" (Ph.D. dissertation, Ball State University, 1965), pp. 87-88.

83. Thornbrough, "Segregation in Indiana During the Klan Era," pp. 594-618.

84. Ibid., p. 617.

85. Indianapolis Board of School Commissioners, *Minutes,* Book DD, November 8, 1927, p. 2.

86. Ibid., Book FF, September 10, 1929, pp. 238-239.

87. Lowe, "Racial Segregation in Indiana," pp. 85-86.

88. *Indianapolis Freeman*, September 5, 1908.

89. Tuttle, *Race Riot*, p. 76.

90. Chicago Commission on Race Relations, *Negro in Chicago*, p. 242.

91. Lieberson, *Ethnic Patterns in American Cities*, p. 122.

92. Mary Jo Herrick, "Negro Employees of the Chicago Board of Education" (M.A. thesis, University of Chicago, 1931), p. 18.

93. Homel, "Negroes in the Chicago Public Schools," p. 43.

94. Chicago Commission on Race Relations, *Negro in Chicago*, p. 242.

95. Ibid.

96. *Chicago Defender*, March 17, 1917.

97. *Chicago Defender*, October 5, 1918.

98. Chicago Commission on Race Relations, *Negro in Chicago*, p. 255.

99. Ibid., p. 253.

100. Chicago Board of Education *Proceedings*, June 9, 1926, p. 1656; June 23, 1926, p. 1779.

101. Chicago Commission on Race Relations, *Negro in Chicago*, p. 254.

102. *Chicago Defender*, August 17, 1918.

103. Ibid.

104. Ibid.

105. *Chicago Tribune*, April 6, 1917.

106. Homel, "Negroes in the Chicago Public Schools," pp. 53-55.

107. *Chicago Defender*, November 13, 1926.

108. *Chicago Defender*, July 9, 1927.

109. *Chicago Tribune*, September 21, 1928, September 22, 1928, September 25, 1928; *Chicago Defender*, October 13, 1928.

110. *Chicago Defender*, April 6, 1929.

111. Herrick, "Negro Employees," p. 18.

112. Homel, "Negroes in the Chicago Public Schools," pp. 103-104.

113. Herrick, "Negro Employees," p. 32.

114. Ibid., p. 9.

115. Harold Baron, "History of Chicago School Segregation to 1953," *Integrated Education* 1 (January 1963): 17.

116. Tuttle, *Race Riot*, p. 76.

CONCLUSION

The historical effect of the school on the pursuit of equality is a critical issue in the evaluation of American education. In 1965, the Committee on the Role of Education in American History, established by the Ford Foundation, emphasized that investigations of the schooling provided for underprivileged Americans—especially those whose "skin [was] not white"— were vital to a final assessment of education.[1] Analyses of the school's policy toward Negroes can be an acid test for an ultimate evaluation of education's influence on egalitarianism because such studies, according to Robert Church, "can provide . . . opportunities to watch the educational establishment stumble badly and to analyze the weaknesses of that establishment revealed thereby—weaknesses that American affluence, openness, and expansionism have generally rendered seemingly harmless and thus invisible."[2]

Since this study has traced Negro education in only three northern cities during the first decades of this century, its conclusions cannot provide an adequate base on which to suggest any comprehensive assessment of the modern school. Such a study, however, does offer certain relevant evidence which may illuminate some of the contours of an evaluation of the role that the twentieth-century urban school has played in the black quest for equality.

The period included in this investigation was important because it witnessed significant movements in American life which affected both the Negro and the school. For the first time, substantial numbers of blacks entered industrial centers in the North and became visible in the cities and the schools. Racial harmony and equality did not characterize this region before the great infusion of blacks during World War I. Jim Crow had stalked the North as well as the South, although his mark on northern states was not as harsh or as total as it was below the Mason-Dixon line. White hostility and discrimination increased and hardened, however, almost in proportion to the expansion of the black population in the North.

An evaluation of early twentieth-century Negro education in the North must center around the response of the schools to this repressive atmosphere. What did educators do to break down prejudice and promote racial tolerance and equality? The evidence from Indianapolis, Chicago, and Philadelphia indicates to the historian that the schools did very little of benefit in this area. Instead, the educational system reflected the attitudes of a prejudiced society by isolating or discriminating against Negro students. A number of officially designated "colored schools" in Philadelphia and a rigid dual system in Indianapolis branded black pupils as inferior. In 1929, the *Philadelphia Tribune* maintained that Jim Crow schools "train white children to believe themselves superior to colored people. They instill in the minds of colored children that they are different—inferior."[3] Chicago administrators did not separate the races by establishing officially segregated schools. However, through extensive granting of transfers and gerrymandering of districts, the consequences of residential segregation were augmented, and all-black and all-white schools became common. Generally, substandard facilities for blacks accompanied racial separation and also reflected the Negro student's inferior social position. Children who attended mixed schools seldom escaped the stigma of separation. Teachers and administrators separated Negro students in the school, the classroom, certain sports, and social activities.

The lack of employment opportunity for middle-class blacks in the economic sphere was also mirrored in school hiring practices. No jobs in mixed schools were available to black educators in Indianapolis and Philadelphia, and in Chicago Negro teachers received only minimal opportunity to teach in the city's schools. In connection with this hiring policy, one must recognize the position of some Negroes who sanctioned segregated schools. They supported this separation not necessarily because they believed it was the ideal arrangement for Negroes, but rather because they wanted to gain some benefits for the black middle class in the educational bureaucracy which systematically rejected black teachers in mixed schools.

On the basis of this study, the racial discrimination and segregation in education cannot be termed an aberration produced by white supremacist groups like the Ku Klux Klan or the Chicago Hyde Park Improvement Protective Club. Discriminatory policies emanated from the mainstream educators and civic leaders in all three cities. Men like Martin Grove Brumbaugh, superintendent of the Philadelphia public schools and later governor of Pennsylvania, and Max Loeb, member of the Chicago Board of Education and prominent businessman, supported segregation. Organizations with no Klan affiliations, such as the Indianapolis Board of School Commissioners and the Indianapolis Chamber of Commerce, demanded separation of the races.

Educational policies which discriminated against Negroes were not limited to those practices specifically directed at black students. Programs which worked against equality were inherent in the new twentieth-century school which emerged during these three decades. The modern school represented a significant shift from the nineteenth-century common school with its uniform curriculum and limited clientele. New compulsory education laws produced universal education and suggested greater commitment by the schools to democratic principles. In fact, an opposite commitment occurred. The goal of the twentieth-century school was not equal education for all but class education for a heterogeneous student population. The educators' justifications for this policy were couched in terms of education which would be appropriate to the individual's ability as well as the community's needs.

The varied curriculum and tracking were integral parts of this re-orientation of the school. The idea of differentiated programs for children coming into the school from widely divergent backgrounds was not inherently antithetical to equality. Experimental programs in the 1960s and 1970s which attempted to remove some of the burdens which handicapped poor children in learning indicated that pupils who experienced brutal environmental conditions did need supplemental programs. But the goal of early twentieth-century educators was not to minimize existing differences between students: they introduced programs which not only acknowledged the differences between pupils but also perpetuated the existing inequality. Pedagogical reforms such as the use of intelligence testing and ability groupings frequently did not measure and label native ability—they assessed past socioeconomic advantages. Ability groupings and the differentiated curriculum channeled lower class blacks and whites into diluted academic programs or vocational education courses which often implicitly rejected the premise "literacy is the most important skill of all."[4]

With the exception of intelligence testing, these educational reforms produced few outcries from the white or black community in the 1920s. Nonetheless, they were clear examples of the manner in which educators actively buttressed social class stratification. Not until 1967 did a court condemn the channeling of students by ability when U.S. Circuit Judge Skelly Wright decreed:

> Even in concept the track system is undemocratic and dis-
> criminatory. Its creator admits it is designed to prepare some
> children for white-collar, and other children for blue-collar
> jobs. Considering the tests used to determine which children
> should receive the blue-collar special, and which the white,
> the danger of children completing their education wearing the
> wrong collar is far too great for this democracy to tolerate.[5]

Negro, as well as lower class, native white and immigrant, children were the victims of these policies. Thus, one must recognize how Negroes were often "miseducated" not only because of policies designed specifically for them, but also because of general educational developments in the early twentieth century which discriminated against virtually all lower class children. In many ways, black education did not embody separate strategies, just as black students did not represent separate problems.

The movement of schools to expand their social services to deal with the environmental problems of children of poverty did not significantly alter the effect of the modern school on lower class students. Particularly with the Negro, these ameliorative efforts were too negligible and the com- mitment too slight to lessen existing inequalities.

In the late 1930s, Doxey Wilkerson stated, "The predominating pattern of educational opportunity in America is consistent with, and tends to aggravate, the gross inequalities which inhere in the nation's social and economic structure."[6] Such a judgment was not consonant with prevailing white views of the schools nor with northern Negroes' faith in the re- generative power of American education. But the schooling of Negroes in Chicago, Indianapolis, and Philadelphia lends credence to this pessimistic appraisal. The black educational experience in these three cities in the early twentieth century also suggests that the crisis in slum schools is not of recent origin; it is one merely of recent discovery and acknowledgment.

NOTES

1. Committee on the Role of Education in American History, *Education and American History* (New York: The Fund for the Advancement of Education, 1965), p. 22.

2. Robert L. Church, "Review of Henry Allen Bullock's *A History of Negro Education in the South*," *Harvard Educational Review* 38 (Fall 1968): 775.

3. *Philadelphia Tribune*, July 18, 1929.

4. Charles E. Silberman, *Crisis in Black and White* (New York: Vintage Books, 1964), p. 254.

5. *Hobson* v. *Hansen*, Civil Action, No. 82-66, *Federal Supplement*, V. 269, p. 515.

6. Wilkerson, "The Negro in American Education" (Manuscript for the Myrdal Study), p. 34.

BIBLIOGRAPHY

PRIMARY SOURCES

MANUSCRIPT COLLECTIONS

Chicago. George Cleveland Hall Branch of the Chicago Public Library. "The Negro in Illinois." A file of reports and interviews compiled by the Illinois Writers Project of the Works Progress Administration.

New York City. Wilkerson, Doxey A. "The Negro in American Education." Manuscript material used in preparation of Gunnar Myrdal's *An American Dilemma*. Schomberg Collection, New York City Public Library.

Philadelphia. Pennsylvania Historical Society. Archives. Jacob C. White, Jr., Papers.

Washington, D.C. Library of Congress. Archives. National Association for the Advancement of Colored People Papers.

PUBLIC DOCUMENTS, EDUCATIONAL SURVEYS, AND ANNUAL REPORTS

Chicago Board of Education. *Annual Report.* 1900-1930.
_____. *Report of Social Centers in the Chicago Public Schools.* 1912.

Chicago Public Schools. *Report of Child Study and Physical Examination of Teachers.* 1928-1929.

Commonwealth of Pennsylvania, Department of Welfare. *Negro Survey of Pennsylvania.* Harrisburg, Pa.: Department of Welfare, 1927.

Greathouse v. Board of School Commissioners of City of Indianapolis. 198 Ind. 95-107. 1926.

Hobson v. *Hansen.* Civil Action, No. 82-66. *Federal Supplement.* V. 269.

Hughes, Elizabeth A. *Living Conditions for Small-Wage Earners in Chicago.* Chicago: Department of Public Welfare, Bureau of Social Surveys, 1925.

Indiana State Board of Education. *Report of the Indianapolis, Indiana, Survey for Vocational Education. Educational Bulletin* No. 21. 1917.

Indianapolis Board of School Commissioners. *Annual Report.* 1879, 1900-1930.

————. *Minutes.* 1894-1930.

Journal of the Common Council of the City of Indianapolis, Indiana, from January 1, 1926, to December 1, 1926. Indianapolis: City of Indianapolis, 1927.

National Association for the Advancement of Colored People. *Annual Report.* 1913-1930.

National Education Association. *Report of the Committee on the Place of Industries in Public Education.* 1910.

Pennsylvania State Department of Public Instruction. *Report of the Survey of the Public Schools of Philadelphia.* 4 books. Philadelphia: Public Education and Child Labor Association of Pennsylvania, 1922.

Philadelphia Board of Public Education. Complete *Minutes.* 1900-1930.

————. *Journal.* 1900-1930.

Philadelphia Public Schools. *Annual Report of the Superintendent of Public Schools.* 1900-1930.

Strayer, George D. *Report of the Survey of the Schools of Chicago, Illinois.* 4 vols. New York: Bureau of Publications, Teachers College, Columbia University, 1932.

U.S. Bureau of the Census. *Eleventh Census of the United States, 1890: Population.* Vol. 1.

————. *Twelfth Census of the United States, 1900: Population.* Vol. 1, Part 1.

————. *Thirteenth Census of the United States, 1910: Population.* Vol. 1, Part 1.

————. *Fourteenth Census of the United States, 1920: Population.* Vol. 2.

————. *Abstract of the Fifteenth Census of the United States, 1930.*

————. *Fifteenth Census of the United States, 1930: Population.* Vol. 4.

————. *Negro Population in the United States, 1790-1915.* Washington, D.C.: U.S. Government Printing Office, 1918.

————. *Negroes in the United States, 1920-1932.* Washington, D.C.: U.S. Government Printing Office, 1935.

————. *Negroes in the United States.* Bulletin 8, 1904.

NEWSPAPERS

Broad Ax (Chicago). 1900-1905.
Chicago Defender. 1909-1930.
Chicago Record Herald. October-November 1909.
Chicago Tribune. 1905-1908; April 1917.
Chicago Whip. 1918-1920.
Indianapolis Freeman. 1900-1930.
Indianapolis Recorder. 1919-1920; 1928.
Inter-Ocean (Chicago). 1902-1908.
New York Age. 1901-1908.
Philadelphia Public Ledger. August 13, 1897.
_____. December 2, 1896.
Philadelphia Tribune. 1912-1930.

WRITINGS BY EDUCATORS, CIVIC LEADERS, AND
REFORMERS OF THE EARLY TWENTIETH CENTURY

BOOKS

Abbott, Edith, and Breckinridge, Sophonisba. *Truancy and Non-attendance in the Chicago Schools.* Chicago: University of Chicago Press, 1917.
Baker, Ray Stannard. *Following the Color Line.* New York: Doubleday, Page and Co., 1908.
Binder, Carroll. *Chicago and the New Negro.* Chicago: *Chicago Daily News,* 1927.
Blascoer, Frances. *Colored School Children in New York.* New York: Public Education Association of the City of New York, 1915.
Bowen, Louise DeKoven. *The Colored People of Chicago.* Chicago: Juvenile Protective Association, 1913.
Boyer, Philip Albert. *The Adjustment of a School to Individual and Community Needs.* Philadelphia: By the Author, 1920.
Chicago Commission on Race Relations. *The Negro in Chicago: A Study of Race Relations and a Race Riot.* Chicago: University of Chicago Press, 1922.
Counts, George S. *School and Society in Chicago.* New York: Harcourt, Brace and Co., 1928.
Cubberley, Ellwood P. *Changing Conceptions of Education.* Boston: Houghton Mifflin Co., 1909.
_____. *State and County Educational Reorganization.* New York: Macmillan Co., 1914.

Dewey, John, and Dewey, Evelyn. *Schools of Tomorrow.* New York: E. P. Dutton and Co., 1915.

DuBois, W.E.B., ed. *The Negro Common School.* Atlanta, Ga.: University Press, 1901.

――――. *The Philadelphia Negro.* University of Pennsylvania Series in Political Economy and Public Law, No. 14. Philadelphia: University of Pennsylvania, 1899.

Dunn, Jacob Piatt. *Greater Indianapolis.* Vol. 1. Chicago: Lewis Publishing Co., 1910.

Hall, G. Stanley. *Adolescence.* Vol. 2. 2 vols. New York: D. Appleton, 1904.

Klineberg, Otto. *Negro Intelligence and Selective Migration.* New York: Columbia University Press, 1935.

Philadelphia Public Education Association. *A Generation of Progress in Our Public Schools, 1881-1912.* Philadelphia: Public Education Association of Philadelphia, 1914.

Terman, Lewis M. *Intelligence Tests and School Reorganization.* New York: World Book Co., 1923.

――――. *The Measurement of Intelligence.* Boston: Houghton Mifflin Co., 1916.

Wood, Junius B. *The Negro in Chicago.* Chicago: *Chicago Daily News,* 1917.

Woofter, Thomas J. *Negro Problems in the Cities.* New York: Doubleday, Doran and Co., 1928.

Wright, Richard R., Jr. *The Negro in Pennsylvania: A Study in Economic History.* Philadelphia: AME Book Concern, Printers, 1912.

Young, Marechal-Neil E. *Some Sociological Aspects of Vocational Guidance of Negro Children.* Philadelphia: By the Author, 1944.

ARTICLES

Anderson, Matthew. "The Berean School of Philadelphia and the Industrial Efficiency of the Negro." *Annals of the American Academy of Political and Social Science* 32 (January 1909): 111-118.

Bean, R. B. "Some Racial Peculiarities of the Negro Brain." *American Journal of Anatomy* 5 (September 1906): 353-433.

Beckham, Albert Sidney. "A Study of Race Attitudes in Negro Children of Adolescent Age." *Journal of Abnormal and Social Psychology* 29 (April-June 1934): 18-29.

Bousfield, Maudelle B. "The Intelligence of Negro Children." *Journal of Negro Education* 1 (October 1932): 388-395.

Buckley, William L. "The School as a Social Center." *Charities* 15 (October 7, 1905): 76-78.

Chivers, Walter R., and Bickford, Mabel E. "Overage Negro Children," *Opportunity* 2 (May 1924): 149-151.

"Cities Reporting the Use of Homogeneous Groupings, the Winnetka Technique and the Dalton Plan." *City School Leaflet,* No. 22. Washington, D.C.: U.S. Bureau of Education, December 1926.

Comstock, Alzada P. "Chicago Housing Conditions; VI: The Problem of the Negro." *American Journal of Sociology* (Chicago) 18 (September 1912): 241-257.

Cornman, Oliver P. "The Retardation of the Pupils of Five City School Systems." *Psychological Clinic* 1 (1907-1908): 245-257.

Crisis (1910 through 1935).

Deffenbaugh, W. S. "Research Bureaus in City School Systems." *City School Leaflet,* No. 5. Washington, D.C.: U.S. Bureau of Education, January 1923.

_____. "Uses of Intelligence and Achievement Tests in 215 Cities." *City School Leaflet,* No. 20. Washington, D.C.: U.S. Bureau of Education, March 1925.

DuBois, W.E.B. "The Black Vote of Philadelphia." *Charities* 15 (October 7, 1905): 31-35.

_____. "Does the Negro Need Separate Schools." *Journal of Negro Education* 4 (July 1935): 328-335.

Eliot, Charles W. "Educational Reform and the Social Order." *School Review* 17 (April 1909): 217-222.

_____. "Industrial Education as an Essential Factor in Our Nation's Prosperity." National Society for the Promotion of Industrial Education, *Bulletin No. 5* (1908): 9-14.

Geyer, Denton L. "Can We Depend upon the Results of Group Intelligence Tests?" *Chicago Schools Journal* 4 (February 1922): 203-210.

Hall, G. Stanley. "The Negro in Africa and America." *Pedagogical Seminary* 12 (September 1905): 350-368.

Harris, William Torrey. "The Education of the Negro." *Atlantic Monthly* 69 (June 1892): 721-736.

Hayes, George. "Vocational Education and the Negro." National Society for the Promotion of Industrial Education, *Bulletin No. 24* (1917): 71-74.

Jenkins, N. C. "What Chance Has the Trained Student." *The Negro in Chicago, 1779-1929*. Chicago: Washington Intercollegiate Club of Chicago, 1929.

McDougald, Elise Johnson. "The School and Its Relation to the Vocational Life of the Negro." *Hospital Social Service* 8 (1923): 218-225.

Mall, F. B. "On Several Anatomical Characteristics of the Human Brain Said to Vary According to Race and Sex." *American Journal of Anatomy* 9 (February 1909): 1-32.

Mayo, M. J. "The Mental Capacity of the American Negro." *Archives of Psychology* 28 (1913): 1-70.

Merrill, Letitia Fyffe. "Children's Choices of Occupations." *Chicago Schools Journal* 5 (December 1922): 154-160.

Miller, Kelly. "The Economic Handicap of the Negro in the North." *Annals of the American Academy of Political and Social Science* 27 (June 1906): 543-550.

Morton-Finney, J. "Negro Educators for Negro Education." *School and Society* 24 (November 20, 1926): 625-629.

Mossell, Sadie T. "The Standard of Living Among One Hundred Negro Migrant Families in Philadelphia." *Annals of the American Academy of Political and Social Science* 98 (November 1921): 173-222.

Odum, Howard W. "Negro Children in the Public Schools of Philadelphia." *Annals of the American Academy of Political and Social Science* 49 (September 1913): 186-208.

Phillips, Byron A. "Retardation in the Elementary Schools of Philadelphia." *Psychological Clinic* 6 (May 15, 1912): 79-90, 107-21.

Ramsey, Andrew William. "The Hoosier Negro Teacher." *Indiana Social Studies Quarterly* 18 (Spring 1964): 37-42.

Rice, J. M. "The Public Schools of St. Louis and Indianapolis." *Forum* 14 (December 1892): 429-444.

Rogers, Don C. "Retardation from the Mental Standpoint." *Chicago Schools Journal* 9 (April 1927): 302-303.

Russell, James E. "The Trend in American Education." *Educational Review* 32 (November 1906): 28-41.

Scott, Emmett J. "Letters of Negro Migrants of 1916-1918." *Journal of Negro History* 4 (October 1919): 412-465.

Shortridge, A. C. "The Schools of Indianapolis." *Indiana Magazine of History* 8 (June 1912): 122-131.

"The Stanford Revision and Extension of the Binet Tests." *Chicago Schools Journal* 2 (December 1919): 9.

Thorndike, Edward L. "Intelligence and Its Uses." *Harper's Monthly Magazine* 140 (January 1920): 227-235.

_____. "Intelligence Scores of Colored Pupils in High Schools." *School and Society* 18 (November 10, 1923): 569-570.

Williams, Fannie Barrier. "Social Bonds in the 'Black Belt' of Chicago." *Charities* 15 (October 5, 1905): 40-44.

UNPUBLISHED SOURCES

Brodhead, John Henry. "Educational Achievement and Its Relation to the Socio-Economic Status of the Negro." Ph.D. dissertation, Temple University, 1937.

Coleman, Julian Dorster. "Are Out of Town Children Responsible for the Retardation in the Colored Schools of Indianapolis, Indiana?" M.A. thesis, University of Chicago, 1924.

Daniels, Virginia. "Attitudes Affecting the Occupational Affiliation of Negroes." Ph.D. dissertation, University of Pittsburgh, 1938.

Herrick, Mary Jo. "Negro Employees of the Chicago Board of Education." M.A. thesis, University of Chicago, 1931.

Smith, Iva Evelyn. "Selected Case Studies of Dependent Negro Children in Their Relationship to the Public School: A Study of the Records of a Child Placing Agency." M.A. thesis, University of Chicago, 1932.

Spears, Frederick W. "The James Forten School: An Experiment in Social Regeneration Through Elementary Manual Training." Paper presented to the Civic Club of Philadelphia, March 2, 1911.

Thompson, Charles Henry. "A Study of the Reading Accomplishments of Colored and White Children." M.A. thesis, University of Chicago, 1920.

Wright, Richard R., Jr. "The Industrial Condition of Negroes in Chicago." B.D. dissertation, University of Chicago, 1901.

Interview with Mrs. Marion Minton at her home, Germantown, Pennsylvania, January 29, 1972.

SECONDARY SOURCES

BOOKS

Bond, Horace Mann. *Education of the Negro in the American Social Order.* New York: Prentice Hall, 1934.

Brown, G. Gordon. *Law Administration in Negro-White Relations in Phila-*

delphia. Philadelphia: Bureau of Municipal Research of Philadelphia, 1947.

Bullough, William A. *Cities and Schools in the Gilded Age*. Port Washington, N.Y.: Kennikat Press, 1974.

Committee on the Role of Education in American History. *Education and American History*. New York: The Fund for the Advancement of Education, 1965.

Cremin, Lawrence. *The Transformation of the School: Progressivism in American Education, 1876-1957*. New York: Alfred A. Knopf, 1962.

Davis, Allen F. *Spearheads for Reform*. New York: Oxford University Press, 1967.

————, and Haller, Mark H., eds. *The Peoples of Philadelphia: A History of Ethnic Groups and Lower-Class Life, 1790-1940*. Philadelphia: Temple University Press, 1973.

Detweiler, Frederick G. *The Negro Press in the United States*. Chicago: University of Chicago Press, 1922.

Drake, St. Clair, and Cayton, Horace. *Black Metropolis*. New York: Harcourt, Brace and Co., 1945.

Drost, Walter H. *David Snedden and Education for Social Efficiency*. Madison: University of Wisconsin Press, 1967.

Epstein, Abraham. *The Negro Migrant to Pittsburgh*. Pittsburgh: University of Pittsburgh Press, 1918.

Fee, Edward Meredith. *The Origin and Growth of Vocational Industrial Education in Philadelphia to 1917*. Philadelphia: Westbrook Publishing Co., 1938.

Flanner House. *The Indianapolis Story*. Indianapolis: n.p., 1939.

Foreman, Clark. *Environmental Factors in Negro Elementary Education*. New York: W. W. Norton and Co., 1932.

Gillard, John T. *The Catholic Church and the American Negro*. Baltimore: St. Joseph's Society Press, 1929.

Gosnell, Harold F. *Negro Politicians*. 2nd ed. Chicago: University of Chicago Press, 1967.

Greer, Colin. *Cobweb Attitudes*. New York: Teachers College Press, Columbia University, 1970.

————. *The Great School Legend*. New York: Basic Books, 1972.

Gutman, Herbert. *The Black Family in Slavery and Freedom, 1750-1925*. New York: Vintage Books, 1977.

Hardin, Clara A. *The Negroes of Philadelphia: The Cultural Adjustment of a Minority Group*. Bryn Mawr, Pa.: By the Author, 1945.

Harlan, Louis R. *Separate and Unequal.* New York: Atheneum, 1968.

Herrick, Mary Jo. *Chicago Schools: A Social and Political History.*
Beverly Hills, Calif.: Sage Publishing Co., 1971.

Higham, John. *Strangers in the Land: Patterns of American Nativism,
1860-1925.* Rutgers, N.J.: Rutgers University Press, 1955.

Hirshon, Stanley P. *Farewell to the Bloody Shirt: Northern Republicans
and the Southern Negro, 1877-1893.* Bloomington: Indiana University
Press, 1962.

Jackson, Kenneth T. *The Ku Klux Klan in the City, 1915-1930.* New York:
Oxford University Press, 1967.

Karier, Clarence J., ed. *Shaping the American Educational State: 1900 to
the Present.* New York: Free Press, 1975.

_____; Violas, Paul C.; and Spring, Joel, eds. *Roots of Crisis: American
Education in the Twentieth Century.* Chicago: Rand McNally and Co.,
1973.

Katz, Michael B. *Class, Bureaucracy and Schools.* New York: Praeger
Publishers, 1971.

_____, ed. *Education in American History.* New York: Praeger Publishers,
1973.

Lazerson, Marvin, and Grubb, W. Norton, eds. *American Education and
Vocationalism: A Documentary History, 1870-1970.* Classics in Education, No. 48. New York: Teachers College Press, 1974.

Lieberson, Stanley. *Ethnic Patterns in American Cities.* New York: Free
Press of Glencoe, 1963.

Litwack, Leon F. *North of Slavery: The Negro in the Free States, 1790-
1860.* Chicago: University of Chicago Press, 1961.

Lyda, John W. *The Negro in the History of Indiana.* Terre Haute: Indiana
Negro History Society, 1953.

Meier, August. *Negro Thought in America 1880-1915.* Ann Arbor: University of Michigan Press, 1963.

_____, and Rudwick, Elliott. *From Plantation to Ghetto.* Rev. ed. New
York: Hill and Wang, 1970.

Perkinson, Henry J. *The Imperfect Panacea: American Faith in Education,
1865-1965.* New York: Random House, 1968.

Pierce, Bessie Louise. *History of Chicago.* Vol. 3. New York: Alfred A.
Knopf, 1957.

Rabb, Kate Milner, and Herschell, William, eds. *An Account of Indianapolis
and Marion County.* Vol. 3 of *History of Indiana.* Edited by Logan
Esarey. 4 vols. Dayton, Ohio: Dayton Historical Publishing Co., 1924.

Ross, Dorothy. *G. Stanley Hall, The Psychologist as Prophet.* Chicago: University of Chicago Press, 1972.

Rugg, Harold. *That Men May Understand.* New York: Doubleday, Doran and Co., 1941.

Ryan, William. *Blaming the Victim.* New York: Vintage Books, 1971.

Saunders, John A. *One Hundred Years After Emancipation: History of the Philadelphia Negro, 1787-1963.* Philadelphia: *Philadelphia Tribune,* 1963.

Schwebel, Milton. *Who Can Be Educated?* New York: Grove Press, 1968.

Silberman, Charles E. *Crisis in Black and White.* New York: Vintage Books, 1964.

Simpson, George Eaton. *The Negro in the Philadelphia Press.* Philadelphia: University of Pennsylvania Press, 1936.

Spear, Allan H. *Black Chicago: The Making of a Negro Ghetto, 1890-1920.* Chicago: University of Chicago Press, 1967.

Spero, Sterling D., and Harris, Abram L. *The Black Worker.* New York: Columbia University Press, 1931.

Taeuber, Karl E., and Taeuber, Alma F. *Negroes in Cities: Residential Segregation and Neighborhood Change.* Chicago: Aldine Publishing Co., 1965.

Thornbrough, Emma Lou. *The Negro in Indiana Before 1900.* Indianapolis: Indiana Historical Bureau, 1957.

Tuttle, William M., Jr. *Race Riot: Chicago in the Red Summer of 1919.* New York: Atheneum, 1972.

Tyack, David B. *The One Best System: A History of American Urban Education.* Cambridge, Mass.: Harvard University Press, 1974.

Voegeli, Jacque. *Free But Not Equal.* Chicago: University of Chicago Press, 1967.

Warner, Sam Bass, Jr. *The Private City.* Philadelphia: University of Pennsylvania Press, 1968.

Wood, Forrest G. *Black Scare: The Racist Response to Emancipation and Reconstruction.* Berkeley: University of California Press, 1968.

X, Malcolm. *The Autobiography of Malcolm X.* New York: Grove Press, 1966.

ARTICLES

Baron, Harold. "History of Chicago School Segregation to 1953." *Integrated Education* 1 (January 1965): 17-19.

_____. "Northern Segregation as a System: The Chicago Schools." *Integrated Education* 3 (December-January 1965-1966): 54-58.

Bunche, Ralph J. "Negro Political Laboratories." *Opportunity* (December 1928): 370-373.

Church, Robert L. "Review of Henry Allen Bullock's *A History of Negro Education in the South.*" *Harvard Educational Review* 38 (Fall 1968): 773-776.

Clark, Kenneth B. "Clash of Cultures in the Classroom." *Integrated Education* 1 (August 1963): 7-14.

Cohen, Sol. "The Industrial Education Movement, 1906-17." *American Quarterly* 20 (Spring 1968): 95-110.

Frazier, E. Franklin. "Problems of Negro Children and Youth." *Journal of Negro Education* 19 (Summer 1950): 269-277.

Greer, Colin. "Immigrants, Negroes and the Public Schools." *Urban Review* 2 (January 1969): 9-12.

Hayres, George Edmund. "Conditions Among Negroes in the Cities." *Annals of the American Academy of Political and Social Science* 98 (November 1921): 173-222.

Hays, Samuel P. "The Politics of Reform in Municipal Government in the Progressive Era." *Pacific Northwest Quarterly* 55 (October 1964): 157-169.

Hershberg, Theodore. "Free Blacks in Antebellum Philadelphia: A Study of Ex-Slaves, Freeborn, and Socio-economic Decline." *Journal of Social History* 4 (Summer 1971): 333-356.

Katz, Michael B. "Comment on Urban Education Symposium." *History of Education Quarterly* 9 (Fall 1969): 326-328.

Meeks, Sylvia. "Philadelphia Works for Integration." *Integrated Education* 2 (April-May 1964): 30-33.

Osofsky, Gilbert. "The Enduring Ghetto." *Journal of American History* 55 (September 1968): 243-255.

Payne, E. George. "Negroes in the Public Elementary Schools of the North." *Annals of the American Academy of Political and Social Science* 130 (November 1928): 224-233.

Stemons, James S. "The Industrial Color-Line in the North." *Century Illustrated Magazine* 60 (July 1900): 477-478.

Thornbrough, Emma Lou. "Segregation in Indiana During the Klan Era of the 1920s." *Mississippi Valley Historical Review* 48 (March 1961): 594-618.

Tyack, David. "Bureaucracy and the Common School: The Example
of Portland, Oregon, 1851-1913." *American Quarterly* 19 (Fall 1967):
457-498.

Wiebe, Robert. "The Social Function of Public Education." *American
Quarterly* 21 (Summer 1969): 147-164.

UNPUBLISHED SOURCES

Franklin, Vincent P. "Educating an Urban Black Community: The Case of
Philadelphia, 1900-1950." Ph.D. dissertation, University of Chicago,
1975.

Heavenridge, Ruth Knapp. "A History of Special Education for the Mentally
Retarded in the Indianapolis Public Schools." M.S. thesis, Indiana
University, 1935.

Homel, Michael Wallace. "Negroes in the Chicago Public Schools, 1910-
1941." Ph.D. dissertation, University of Chicago, 1972.

Issel, William Henry. "Schools for a Modern Age: Educational Reform
in Pennsylvania in the Progressive Era." Ph.D. dissertation, University
of Pennsylvania, 1969.

Jerrems, Raymond L. "A Sociological-Educational Study of a Public
School in a Negro Lower-Class Area of a Big City." Ph.D. dissertation,
University of Chicago, 1965.

Karier, Clarence J. "Ideology and Evaluation: In Quest of Meritocracy."
Paper prepared for the Wisconsin Conference on Education and Evaluation, University of Wisconsin, Madison, April 26-27, 1973.

Lowe, Robert Allen. "Racial Segregation in Indiana, 1920-1950." Ph.D.
dissertation, Ball State University, 1965.

MacLean, Hazel C. "Evolution of the Philadelphia School System Since
the Year 1818." M.A. thesis, Temple University, 1930.

Marks, Russell. "Testers, Trackers and Trustees: The Ideology of the
Intelligence Testing Movement in America, 1900-1954." Ph.D. dissertation, University of Illinois, 1972.

Mason, Mame Charlotte. "The Policy of Segregation in the Public Schools
of Ohio, Indiana, and Illinois." M.A. thesis, University of Chicago,
1917.

Miller, James Erroll. "The Negro in Pennsylvania Politics with Special
Reference to Philadelphia Since 1932." Ph.D. dissertation, University
of Pennsylvania, 1945.

Nelson, H. Viscount, Jr. "Race and Class Consciousness of Philadelphia Negroes with Special Emphasis on the Years Between 1927 and 1940." Ph.D. dissertation, University of Pennsylvania, 1969.

Porter, Jennie D. "Problems of Negro Education in Northern and Border Cities." Ph.D. dissertation, University of Cincinnati, 1928.

Rhodes, Helen Louise. "Negro Segregation in Indiana." M.A. thesis, Butler University, 1935.

Silcox, Harry Charles. "A Comparative Study in School Desegregation, The Boston and Philadelphia Experience, 1800-1881." Ph.D. dissertation, Temple University, 1972.

INDEX

About the Author

Judy Jolley Mohraz is assistant professor of history at Southern Methodist University in Dallas, Texas. Her academic specialty is American intellectual history.